ENIGMATIC MISTS

Enigmatic Mists

Echoes Across Continents

SAM LORAY

Mohammed Altaf Hussain

Contents

Table of Content

4.2 Examining how mist transforms the vast dunes and ancient land-scapes.
4.3 Stories of nomadic cultures and their relationship with desert mists.

Chapter 5: Frozen Whispers: Arctic Mist in Scandinavia:
5.1 Navigating the chilling beauty of mist in Scandinavia.
5.2 Examining mist's role in the unique ecosystems of the Arctic Circle.
5.3 Tales of northern lights and misty fjords.

Chapter 6: Pacific Islands: Veiled Paradises:
6.1 Embracing the tropical allure of mist in Pacific island destinations.
6.2 Exploring misty jungles, volcanic landscapes, and hidden waterfalls.
6.3 Cultural stories of mist as a bridge between nature and spirituality.

Chapter 7: Ancient Mysteries of Asian Temples:
7.1 Concluding the journey with the mystical mists surrounding Asian temples.
7.2 Examining the symbolic and spiritual significance of mist in Asian cultures.
7.3 Reflecting on the echoes of mist across diverse continents.

Introduction

In the ethereal embroidery of our reality, there exists a peculiarity that rises above topographical limits and social scenes — the baffling fogs that shroud our planet's different territories. This investigation takes us on a hypnotizing venture across mainlands, digging into the magical charm of fog, unwinding its social importance, and uncovering the untold stories that reverberation through reality.

The actual pith of fog, with its tricky nature, has been a material whereupon the stories of mankind's set of experiences and normal marvels have been painted. A peculiarity interfaces the farthest reaches of the globe, encompassing scenes in a powerful hug, murmuring mysteries that resound through the ages. As we leave on this odyssey, our most memorable objective lies in the midst of the moving slopes and old palaces of Scotland.

Scotland, a land saturated with fantasy and legend, is covered in the murmuring hazes that dance upon its fields and lochs. These fogs, as ethereal narrators, weave stories of bygone eras, as though the very air conveys reverberations of history. The Scottish fog, with its mysterious quality, turns into an extension between the unmistakable present and the immaterial domains of legends. The fog loaded scenes of Scotland stand demonstration of the getting through association among nature and the human creative mind.

From the foggy slopes of Scotland, our process takes us to the Himalayas, where transcending pinnacles and otherworldly safe-havens are hidden in mysterious covers of fog. In the levels of Nepal, fog takes on a profound importance, as though the very air is accused of the energy of old practices. Journeying across these fog loaded domains turns into an extraordinary encounter, where the limits between the physical and the mystical haze. The Himalayan fog turns into a course for thoughtfulness, interfacing explorers with the otherworldly reverberations of the mountains.

Wandering further, we get ourselves profound inside the core of the Amazon rainforest in Brazil, where fog takes on an alternate job in the coordination of biodiversity. The fog, rising like ringlets through the thick foliage, assumes an essential part in supporting the fragile equilibrium of life in this rich environment. As we explore the cloudy rainforests, we uncover the mysteries of an old domain, where fog turns into the breath of the Earth, supporting the horde types of life that call the Amazon home.

Our process then drives us to the immeasurability of the Sahara Desert in Africa, where the baffling fogs assume an altogether unique personality.

The quiet sands of the Sahara are decorated with the persona of whirling fog, changing the parched scene into a consistently moving material of excellence. Migrant societies that have crossed these ridges for quite a long time share accounts of fog as a buddy in their excursion, a quiet observer to the rhythmic movement of time in the endlessness of the desert.

From the parched deserts, we adventure north to Scandinavia, where frozen murmurs wind through fog covered scenes. The Cold fog, moving over fjords and frozen scenes, portrays tormenting excellence. In this frigid domain, fog turns into a shroud that mellow the cruel edges of the Cold Circle, making a strange and captivating environment. Aurora Borealis flash through the fog, projecting an extraordinary shine over the frozen scenes, making Scandinavia a place that is known for frozen dreams.

As we venture across the Pacific Islands, fog turns into a hidden heaven, winding through tropical wildernesses, volcanic landscapes, and flowing cascades. The foggy scenes of these islands hold social stories that interlace with the normal world, making an amicable connection between the unmistakable and the concealed. Fog turns into an image of recharging and association, a string that attaches the islanders to their genealogical roots and the consistently changing hug of nature.

Our odyssey closes with the old secrets of Asian sanctuaries, where fog takes on a representative and profound importance. The cloudy environmental elements of these sacrosanct locales make a vibe of serenity and adoration, welcoming consideration and thoughtfulness. The fog turns into a channel for profound reflection, wrapping these sanctuaries in an emanation of magic that rises above time.

In the last reverberates of our excursion, we wind up remaining at the junction of landmasses, understanding that fog isn't just a meteorological peculiarity yet a general language that addresses the spirit of humankind. Mysterious fogs, reverberating across landmasses, interface us to the common human experience of marvel and adoration for the inconspicuous. It is an update that, notwithstanding our different societies and scenes, we are bound together by the consistent ideas of nature's excellence and the secrets that wait in its hidden hug. This investigation of confounding fogs fills in as a challenge to see the world through another focal point, one that perceives the interconnectedness of our planet's miracles and the ageless reverberations that resound across its huge and differed scenes.

1. **Setting the stage for the mysterious and universal allure of mist.**
   In the terrific embroidery of our reality, there exists a peculiarity that rises above the limits of time, culture, and topography — a peculiarity that has charmed human creative mind since days of yore. This is the baffling charm of fog, an apparently fleeting cover that covers our scenes, murmuring stories of secret and inspiring a feeling of miracle.
   As we set out on this investigation of fog, it is vital for made way for the significant and widespread interest that this climatic peculiarity holds for mankind.
   Fog, by its actual nature, possesses a domain between the seen and the inconspicuous. A peculiarity challenges simple classification, drifting between the substantial and the elusive, the known and the puzzling. This environmental dance of water drops suspended in air has the ability to change customary scenes into ethereal domains, enchanting that rises above social, geological, and worldly limits.
   The charm of fog lies in its tricky nature — a transitory and consistently changing presence that wraps our environmental elements in an air embrace. Whether it is the moving slopes of Scotland, the transcending pinnacles of the Himalayas, or the thick rainforests of the Amazon, fog loans a powerful quality to the scenes it contacts. Its transient nature makes a climate of steady change, as though the very air is instilled with the wizardry of transformation.
   Socially, fog has been woven into the texture of human folklore and imagery. In endless practices and fables, fog is many times portrayed as a limit between the human domain and the enchanted unexplored world. It turns into an edge through which spirits might pass, a shroud that isolates the customary from the unprecedented. This social importance reverberations across mainlands, appearing in stories that have been gone down through ages, each permeated with a feeling of worship for the secrets hidden inside the fog.
   As we set out on this excursion, perceiving the emotive force of mist

is essential. It isn't only a meteorological peculiarity yet an impetus for a scope of feelings — wonderment, thoughtfulness, and a profound feeling of association with the regular world. The widespread allure of fog lies in its capacity to bring out a feeling of the great, welcoming thought and an acknowledgment of the heavenly in the common. Whether it is the eerie excellence of cloudy Scottish fields or the profound reflections motivated by Himalayan fog, the close to home reverberation of fog rises above social and geological limits.

Besides, fog fills in as a material whereupon light and shadow paint their own magnum opus. The exchange of daylight with the suspended water beads makes a visual ensemble, transforming fog loaded scenes into ethereal works of art that challenge the shows of the customary. This visual verse isn't restricted to a particular district; rather, a peculiarity reverberations across landmasses, every region contributing its own extraordinary stanza to the general sythesis of fog.

In writing and workmanship, fog has been a common theme — an image of equivocalness, progress, and the unexplored world.

From the hazy roads of Victorian London in Charles Dickens' books to the dim scenes deified in the artworks of J.M.W. Turner, specialists and essayists have tried to catch the substance of fog as a representation for the secrets of presence. This creative investigation further supports the all inclusive interest with fog, as it rises above the limits of language and culture to impart a common human encounter.

The persona of fog additionally stretches out to its environmental effect on different scenes. Fog assumes a vital part in supporting environments, from the dampness it gives to bone-dry deserts to the sensitive equilibrium it keeps up with in tropical rainforests. Its impact on verdure is a demonstration of the interconnectedness of the regular world, and as we navigate the landmasses, we will observer how fog shapes and supports the different environments it wraps.

2. Exploring the cultural significance of mist across continents.

In our excursion through the fog loaded scenes that length landmasses, it is basic to dig into the rich embroidery of social importance woven into the actual texture of fog. Fog, past its meteorological embodiment, is a peculiarity that resounds profoundly inside the human mind, taking on different implications and emblematic portrayals across the globe. From the magical fields of Scotland to the otherworldly safe-havens of the Himalayas, the social significance of fog arises as a consistent idea, interfacing different social orders through shared stories and convictions.

Scotland, Where Fog Meets Fantasy:

In the moving slopes and old palaces of Scotland, fog expects a job past the air; it turns into a basic piece of the social and legendary scene. Here, fog isn't just a weather pattern yet a narrator, wrapping the Scottish fields and lochs in an ethereal shroud that obscures the lines among the real world and fables. It is in this fog loaded feeling that legends are conceived, where the very air appears to be pregnant with stories of kelpies, selkies, and antiquated factions. The fog, whirling through the leftovers of palaces and standing stones, turns into a living element, murmuring the adventures of a former time.

Socially, fog in Scotland is a similitude for the concealed and the baffling, mirroring a shared mindset that embraces the mysterious. It fills in as an extension between the unmistakable and the elusive, a peculiarity that obscures the limits between the normal and powerful domains. Through fog, Scotland protects its social legacy, permitting the past to wait in the present, and the fog covered scenes become a material whereupon the aggregate creative mind paints the narratives of the Scottish soul.

Himalayan Levels and Profound Shroud:

As we rise from the hazy fields of Scotland, our process takes us to the transcending pinnacles of the Himalayas, where fog expects an otherworldly meaning of significant greatness.

In the high elevations of Nepal, fog turns into a channel for the heavenly — an unmistakable sign of the concealed powers that shape the otherworldly scene of the locale. Fog, veiling holy mountains and old cloisters, rises above its meteorological definition to turn into an image of the supernatural and the otherworldly.

Socially, fog in the Himalayas is entwined with the otherworldly practices and convictions of the assorted networks that call this locale home. It isn't just a barometrical peculiarity however a consecrated shroud that isolates the unremarkable from the heavenly. Pioneers journey across fog covered mountain passes, and ascetic serenades resound through the ethereal fog, making an environment where the limits between the physical and the powerful disintegrate. Fog in the Himalayas turns into a profound buddy, an aide that drives searchers to the domains of edification and contemplation.

Amazonian Secrets and the Breath of the Earth:

As our process takes us to the Amazon rainforest in Brazil, fog expects an alternate social reverberation — one intently attached to the imperativeness of the normal world. In the thick foliage of the rainforest, fog turns into the breath of the Earth, winding through the dynamic biological system like a daily existence force. The social meaning of fog here lies in its job as a nurturer, a sustainer of life that guarantees the flourishing biodiversity of the district.

Socially, fog in the Amazon is worshipped as a crucial power that interfaces generally living creatures in a fragile equilibrium. Native societies view fog not as an air event but rather as an otherworldly substance — an exemplification of the interconnectedness of every single living thing. Fog loaded mornings in the Amazon become a fellowship with the World's breath, a hallowed dance that propagates the pattern of life. The social meaning of fog in the Amazon in this manner mirrors an amicable connection among humankind and nature, where fog turns into an image of environmental interconnectedness.

African Sands and Migrant Murmurs:

Wandering into the immeasurability of the Sahara Desert in Africa, fog takes on a social importance that repeats the itinerant practices of the locale. Here, fog turns into a buddy in the parched scenes, a transient presence that shapes the lifestyle for those navigating the vast ridges. The social significance of fog in the Sahara lies in its job as a quiet observer to the traveling rhythms of life, a peculiarity that tempers the brutality of the desert.

Socially, fog in the Sahara is entwined with the stories of roaming clans, who explore the moving sands with a cozy comprehension of the fog's subtleties. It turns into an aide in the desert, a hidden way that leads travelers through the limitlessness of the scene. Fog loaded mornings convey accounts of flexibility and variation, where roaming murmurs reverberation through the fog, imparting stories of endurance and beneficial interaction to the always evolving climate.

Scandinavian Ice and Cold Murmurs:

Our process then takes us north to Scandinavia, where fog expects a social importance in the frozen scenes of the Icy Circle. In this frigid domain, fog turns into a quiet narrator, painting the fjords and frozen scenes with an ethereal brush. The social significance of fog in Scandinavia lies in its job as a shaper of the visual and profound scene — a peculiarity that transforms the cruelty of the Cold into a domain of tormenting excellence.

Socially, fog in Scandinavia is commended in workmanship, writing, and old stories as an image of equivocalness and change. It turns into a dream for craftsmen like Edvard Chomp, whose works of art catch the emotive force of fog in the Nordic scene. The social reverberation of fog in Scandinavia mirrors an appreciation for the radiant, where fog loaded mornings become a wellspring of motivation for imagination and examination.

Pacific Islands and Hidden Heavens:

As we navigate the hazy wildernesses and volcanic territories of the Pacific Islands, social importance takes on an alternate tone. Here, fog turns into an image of recharging and association — a peculiarity that winds through tropical scenes and social practices the same. The fog loaded heavens of the Pacific Islands are not just environmental events but rather a demonstration of the cooperative connection among nature and culture.

Socially, fog in the Pacific Islands is weaved with accounts of creation and otherworldliness. It turns into a shroud that isolates the holy from the profane, a vaporous extension that interfaces the unmistakable world with the profound domain. Fog loaded cascades and thick wildernesses become spots of veneration, where social practices and ceremonies unfurl together as one with the fog's delicate hug. The social meaning of fog in the Pacific Islands mirrors a profound regard for nature and an acknowledgment of fog as a course for otherworldly encounters.

Asian Sanctuaries and the Cloak of Serenity:

Our social investigation deduces in the foggy environmental factors of Asian sanctuaries, where fog expects a representative and profound importance. In the fog loaded regions of old sanctuaries, social importance is gotten from the air peculiarity as well as from the quietness it brings. Fog turns into an illustration for internal harmony, a visual portrayal of the serenity looked for through reflection and thought.

Socially, fog in Asian sanctuaries typifies the standards of Harmony reasoning, where straightforwardness and agreement are principal. It turns into a conductor for otherworldly thoughtfulness, making a climate of calm reflection and care. The dim environmental elements of Asian sanctuaries mirror the social comprehension that excellence lies in effortlessness, and that fog, with its delicate veiling of scenes, turns into a sign of peacefulness and otherworldly profundity.

3. Teasing the diverse stories that will unfold.

As we stand at the limit of this captivating excursion through fog loaded scenes, the expectation is tangible, and the air is pregnant with the commitment of different stories that are ready to unfurl. Every objective, with its special social embroidered artwork and climatic subtleties, prods the creative mind with the possibility of disclosing stories that reverberate with the human soul. From the eerie fields of Scotland to the otherworldly levels of the Himalayas, the rich heart of the Amazon, the sweeping Sahara, the cold domains of Scandinavia, the paradisiacal Pacific Islands, and the serene sanctuaries of Asia, the fog turns into a narrator, murmuring privileged insights that navigate reality.

Scotland: An Ensemble of Shadows and Spirits:

In the foggy fields and old palaces of Scotland, an ensemble of shadows and spirits is standing by. The stories that wait in the fog are basically as different as the actual scenes. From the incredible Loch Ness Beast, said to rise out of the fog covered waters, to the otherworldly figures that wind through the vestiges of palaces, fog turns into a medium through which the heavenly and the unremarkable coincide. The hazy scenes of Scotland are not just a scenery but rather a person in these accounts, making way for experiences with the puzzling and the extraordinary.

The fog that covers the Scottish fields turns into a material whereupon the old stories of the land is painted. It hides old standing stones, internment hills, and remainders of failed to remember civic establishments. As we track through the fog, the reverberations of Celtic fantasies and Arthurian legends wait, welcoming us to envision when fog was a meteorological peculiarity as well as a cloak that isolated the everyday from the otherworldly. The different accounts of Scotland's fog uncover a social profundity that rises above the shallow, welcoming us to investigate the transaction between nature, folklore, and the human creative mind.

Himalayas: Pinnacles of Edification and Greatness:

From the mysterious fields of Scotland, our process rises to the transcending pinnacles of the Himalayas — a domain where fog turns into a similitude for edification and greatness. The different stories that unfurl in the slender demeanor of these high elevations are pervaded with otherworldly importance, mirroring the social embroidery of the networks that call the Himalayas home. Fog, here, isn't simply a barometrical peculiarity yet a cloak that isolates the ordinary from the heavenly.

In the shadow of sacrosanct mountains, fog turns into a sidekick on journeys where the physical and the supernatural join. As we cross fog covered mountain passes and visit old religious communities roosted on the edges of bluffs, the narratives that arise discuss profound journeys, edification, and the quest for internal harmony.

The Himalayan fog conveys with it the serenades of priests, the strides of explorers, and the murmurs of sages who looked for comfort in the levels. These different accounts mirror the mind boggling joining of otherworldliness, scene, and social practices in the embroidery of the Himalayas.

Amazon Rainforest: The Breath of Life and Biodiversity:

Slipping from the elevated levels of the Himalayas, our process goes in a new direction as we drench ourselves in the thick foliage of the Amazon rainforest. Here, fog isn't simply a climate peculiarity yet the breath of the actual Earth — an imperative power that supports the exceptional biodiversity of the locale. The different stories that rise out of the core of the Amazon uncover a social importance profoundly weaved with natural concordance and the interconnectedness of every living being.

The fog that moves through the rainforest turns into a course forever, supporting a rich embroidery of vegetation. As we investigate the accounts of native societies and their advantageous connection with the fog loaded scenes, we experience stories that discuss respect for nature, the soul of concurrence, and the significant comprehension of the fragile equilibrium that supports the rainforest biological system. The Amazonian fog isn't just a mechanism for different stories yet a living element that mirrors the social ethos of conservation and regard for the World's breath.

Sahara Desert: Itinerant Murmurs in the Quiet Sands:

Leaving the rich hug of the rainforest, our process drives us to the tremendousness of the Sahara Desert — an apparently desolate scene that harbors an abundance of different stories formed by traveling murmurs and the quiet sands. In this parched domain, fog turns into a valuable sidekick, relaxing the cruelty of the desert and impacting the roaming lifestyle. The accounts that unfurl in the Sahara are not stories of need but rather accounts of transformation, flexibility, and the getting through connection among mankind and the always moving sands.

As we cross the rises hidden in fog, we experience itinerant clans whose accounts are scratched into the immense material of the desert. The Sahara turns into a theater where fog assumes a focal part in the methods for surviving of these wanderers, directing them through the sweeping vacancy and turning into a wellspring of motivation for social articulations, from verse to music. The Sahara's fog uncovers stories of a roaming presence that resists the inhospitality of the desert, mirroring a significant social connection to the consistently evolving scene.

Scandinavia: Frozen Dreams and Frosty Domains:

From the glow of the Sahara, our process takes a turn towards the frozen dreams of Scandinavia. In these cold domains, fog turns into a quiet narrator, painting fjords, backwoods, and mountains with an ethereal touch.

The different stories rising up out of Scandinavia are saturated with a social appreciation for the great, where fog loaded scenes become a wellspring of motivation for specialists, scholars, and narrators the same.

The fog that cloak the Nordic scenes changes the recognizable into the remarkable. In progress of specialists like Edvard Chomp, fog turns into a dream, catching the emotive force of the scene covered in cloak of white.

The social meaning of fog in Scandinavia lies in its capacity to bring out feelings, to challenge discernments, and to welcome thought notwithstanding the frozen excellence that resists the normal. As we investigate these fog loaded scenes, we experience stories that discuss the fragile dance among light and shadow, nature and culture, uncovering a social profundity that embraces the melancholic magnificence of fog.

Pacific Islands: Hidden Heavens and Social Veneration:
Proceeding with our excursion, we end up in the midst of the dim wildernesses and volcanic landscapes of the Pacific Islands — a heaven hidden in fog that mirrors a social love for nature and the otherworldly domain. The narratives that unfurl in these paradisiacal scenes discuss an agreeable connection among humankind and the fog loaded environmental elements, where social practices and customs unfurl working together with the steadily evolving climate.

Fog turns into an image of restoration and association in the Pacific Islands, where cascades and thick wildernesses are spots of social importance. The fog loaded scenes act as settings for creation fantasies, otherworldly encounters, and social articulations that feature the interconnectedness of people with the regular world. Through these different stories, the fog in the Pacific Islands arises as in excess of a meteorological peculiarity — it turns into a course for profound encounters and a sign of the cooperative connection among culture and nature.

Asian Sanctuaries: Fog as Serene Reflection:
Our investigation finishes in the hazy environmental elements of Asian sanctuaries, where social importance is gotten from the climatic peculiarity as well as from the serenity it brings. Fog turns into an illustration for internal harmony, a visual portrayal of the quietness looked for through reflection and thought. The narratives that unfurl in these fog loaded sanctuary regions mirror a social comprehension that magnificence lies in effortlessness, where fog turns into a sign of quietness and profound profundity.

As we dig into the stories of fog covered sanctuaries, we experience stories of otherworldly reflection, care, and the mission for illumination. The fog loaded mood turns into a safe-haven where social practices and customs unfurl as one with the environmental circumstances. Through different accounts of fog kissed sanctuaries, we look into the social qualities that focus on serenity, care, and the quest for inward harmony — a social profundity that hoists fog past its actual sign to an image of profound greatness.

As we stand on the cusp of this vivid excursion through fog loaded scenes, the different stories that bother our creative mind offer a brief look into the social extravagance and profundity that look for us. From the eerie fields of Scotland to the profound levels of the Himalayas, from the life-supporting fog of the Amazon to the traveling murmurs of the Sahara, from the frozen dreams of Scandinavia to the paradisiacal Pacific Islands, and the peaceful sanctuaries of Asia, every objective unfurls a story embroidery that mirrors the harmonious connection between culture, nature, and fog. The different stories, similar to strings woven into the foggy texture of the scenes, welcome us to investigate the social meaning of fog across mainlands and to see the value in the profundity of significance implanted in the steadily changing climatic peculiarity.

Chapter 1

The Whispering Fogs of Scotland

The Murmuring Hazes of Scotland: A Magical Embroidery Revealed

In the core of the Scottish High countries, where old mountains stand sentinel and lochs stretch like dull mirrors, a peculiarity both spooky and enamoring unfurls — the Murmuring Hazes of Scotland. As sunrise breaks and the principal light graces the tough scene, the ethereal fogs ascend from the earth, shrouding the valleys and slopes in an unearthly dance that has hypnotized ages.

These hazes, more than simple meteorological events, convey with them a feeling of supernatural quality, a murmured association with the rich embroidery of Scotland's celebrated past. It is expressed that inside these vaporous cloak, the voices of the actual land reverberation — a chorale of history, legend, and the spirits that stay inside the old stones.

The Murmuring Hazes are not bound to a specific season; rather, they are vaporous guests that emerge with a specific eccentricity. In the cooler months, they float drowsily through the glens, winding between the skeletal parts of antiquated trees and following the shapes of long-neglected palaces. In summer, they take on a milder disposition, waiting over emerald-green scenes and giving a practically fantastical setting to the rich, moving slopes.

The peculiarity's starting points are well established in the topographical and barometrical characteristics of the locale. Scotland's geology, portrayed by rocky pinnacles and profound cold valleys, makes the best circumstances for the arrangement of these murmuring hazes. As temperature differentials between the land and the air happen, dampness loaded air blends into these magical fumes that have come to represent the convergence of the normal and the heavenly.

To observe the Murmuring Hazes is to participate in an excursion through time, as the fogs, as ethereal caretakers, reveal the mysteries that falsehood concealed underneath the outer layer of the land. Legends flourish about ghostly nebulous visions saw through the cover, of High country fighters who once wandered the glens and tragically missing darlings who tracked down comfort in the fogs' hug. These stories, went down through ages, add layers of persona to a generally captivating peculiarity.

Maybe no place is the exchange between the Murmuring Hazes and Scotland's antiquated history more obvious than in the shadow of the solid standing stones that speck the scene. As the fogs twist around these endured sentinels, it is as though the very stones themselves are participated in a quiet discussion with the land. The air becomes accused of an energy that rises above the unmistakable, a demonstration of the getting through association between individuals of Scotland and their celebrated past.

In the distant towns settled inside the folds of the High countries, local people discuss the hazes with a blend of love and commonality. To them, the fogs are not simply meteorological occasions but rather living substances, conductors between the natural domain and the ethereal. Seniors recap stories of antiquated ceremonies performed at the edges of the fog, where the cover between the seen and the inconspicuous is at its most slender.

The Murmuring Hazes are not bound to the land alone; they additionally hold influence over the famous lochs that reflect the agonizing skies above. At sunrise, as the fogs ascend from the still waters, the actual lochs appear to breathe out the mysteries concealed in their profundities. It is a scene of stunning excellence and creepy serenity, where nature's components merge to make a scene that rises above the conventional.

However, for all their persona, the Murmuring Hazes likewise fill a functional need in the Good country environment. As they float through the glens, the fogs present their nurturing dampness to the verdure, supporting the sensitive equilibrium of the environment. The murmurs of the land, conveyed by the hazes, talk of the past as well as of the repeating idea of life and recharging.

In the domain of writing and craftsmanship, the Murmuring Hazes have roused endless works that look to catch the pith of this fleeting peculiarity.

Writers have written sections that reverberation the unpleasant magnificence of the fogs, while painters have looked to reproduce the environmental interchange among light and haze on material. It is a demonstration of the persevering through effect of this regular display on the human creative mind, a wellspring of motivation that rises above social and imaginative limits.

As day goes to night in the Good countries, the Murmuring Hazes go through a change. In the twilight hours, they take on a practically unearthly iridescence, providing reason to feel ambiguous about a powerful gleam the scene. The air turns out to be thick with a feeling of charm, as though the actual texture of the truth is extended dainty within the sight of these tricky fogs.

For the people who adventure into the core of the haze loaded glens, a feeling of immortality wins. The limits among over a wide span of time obscure, and one can nearly hear the reverberations of old strides proceeding with caution on the dew-kissed grass. It is an excursion into the aggregate memory of a land saturated with history, where the Murmuring Hazes act as ethereal narrators, describing stories written in the language of fog and shadow.

The Murmuring Hazes of Scotland are in excess of a meteorological peculiarity; they are an entryway to the spirit of the High countries. As they weave their direction through glens and lochs, encompassing antiquated stones and endured trees, they rejuvenate the tales and legends that have formed this enchanted scene. The murmurs of the land, conveyed by the hazes, reverberation across the hundreds of years, welcoming the people who will tune in into a domain where the conventional and the phenomenal combine in a dance of fog and secret.

1.1 Immersing into the mystique of Scottish mists.

Inundating into the Persona of Scottish Fogs: An Excursion Through Ethereal Cover

Setting out on an excursion into the core of Scotland, one winds up enthralled by the ethereal hug of the enchanted fogs that wind through the scene. These vaporous rings, more than simple meteorological peculiarities, convey with them an unmistakable feeling of sorcery, history, and an old association with the land. To really drench oneself into the persona of Scottish fogs is to set out on an excursion through time and nature, where the normal becomes exceptional and the everyday is changed into the uncommon.

The peculiarity of Scottish fogs isn't bound to a particular season or region; rather, it is a consistently present dance between the components and the scene. Picture the rough High countries, where the murmuring hazes rise like spooky phantoms, darkening the spiked pinnacles and moving slopes. In the chill of morning, as the initial light gets through the cloudy cover, the scene is uncovered in sections — a momentary look into a world that appears to be suspended among the real world and charm.

As one dives further into the High country landscape, the fogs take on a practically aware quality. It is as though the actual soul of Scotland, saturated with hundreds of years of fantasy and legend, inhales through the vaporous shroud. The air becomes accused of a peaceful energy, and the scene changes into a dreamscape where the over a significant time span combine. The murmurs of old stories, conveyed by the fogs, reverberation through the glens, adding layers of secret to the generally captivating environmental factors.

Scotland's geology, described by jagged mountains, peaceful lochs, and thick forests, gives the best material to the appearance of these magical fogs. The temperature differentials between the cool land and the environmental air make the ideal circumstances for the development of the ethereal cloak. It is a dance organized essentially, where dampness loaded air winds through the scene, uncovering and hiding in equivalent measure.

Wandering into the core of the fogs, one ends up wrapped in a universe of transient excellence. Old timberlands, hung in fog, take on an extraordinary tastefulness. Trees, their branches decorated with beads of dampness, stand like sentinels protecting the mysteries of the land. The very earth underneath one's feet appears to resound with an immortal energy — a heartbeat that thumps as one with the rhythmic movement of the ethereal fogs.

Among the most famous pictures related with Scottish fogs are the antiquated standing stones dissipated across the scene. These endured stone monuments, remainders of an age long past, rise up out of the fog like quiet gatekeepers of failed to remember legend. The transaction between the standing stones and the murmuring hazes makes a scene that rises above the visual; it is a combination of the substantial and the immaterial, where the actual stones appear to inhale with the soul of the land.

It is inside this fog covered domain that Scotland's rich history wakes up. The stories of groups, fights, and amazing figures reverberation through the glens, conveyed by the breezes that guide the fogs. The spirits of High country champions and old tribal leaders, it is accepted, track down comfort in the vaporous hug, turning into a necessary piece of the always evolving scene. It is a fellowship between the living and the familial, a string that winds through the actual texture of Scottish character.

The Murmuring Hazes of Scotland are not restricted to light hours; they go through a transformation as the sun sets and night plunges upon the scene. In the delicate shine of evening glow, the fogs take on a practically ethereal iridescence. It is a scene directly from the domains of imagination — a scene washed in brilliant light, where shadows hit the dance floor with the fogs in a nighttime waltz. The air becomes accused of an extraordinary energy, as though the actual embodiment of sorcery is woven into the texture of the evening.

For the people who decide to wander into the Good country fogs during the evening, the experience verges on the strange. The limits between the seen and the concealed haze, and the scene turns into a material whereupon dreams and imaginings show some signs of life. It is the point at which the cover between the unremarkable and the puzzling is at its most slender, and one could get looks at slippery animals from the pages of Celtic legends — an existence where the normal standards of reality give approach to the uncommon.

The effect of the Murmuring Hazes on the social and imaginative embroidery of Scotland is vast. Across hundreds of years, writers, essayists, and craftsmen have tried to catch the pith of this supernatural peculiarity. In the sections of artists like Robert Copies, the fogs are depicted as ethereal dreams, murmuring mysteries to the people who might tune in. Specialists, as well, have been roused by the air interchange among light and haze, making magnum opuses that mirror the slippery magnificence of the Good country scene.

The imaginative articulation stretches out past writing and visual expressions; it is imbued in the very legends and customs of Scotland. The old faith in the "dainty spots," where the limit between the human domain and the powerful is permeable, finds reverberation in the fog covered glens. There one could experience the pixie people or hear the eerie kinds of the bagpipes conveyed by the breeze.

In the curious towns settled inside the folds of the Good countries, local people respect the fogs with a mix of wonderment and commonality. To them, the hazes are not only environmental peculiarities but rather living elements with their very own feeling. Stories flourish of ceremonies performed at the edges of the fog, where the cover between the substantial and the immaterial is penetrated. These ceremonies, gave over through ages, are a demonstration of the getting through association between individuals of Scotland and the enchanted fogs that shape their scene.

The lochs of Scotland, reflected surfaces that mirror the agonizing skies above, likewise assume a critical part in the dance of the Murmuring Hazes. At first light, as the fogs ascend from the still waters, the lochs become a material whereupon the ethereal excellence of the scene is painted. The transaction among water and fog causes a situation of stunning serenity, as though nature itself is participated in a quiet exchange with its own appearance.

One can't examine the persona of Scottish fogs without recognizing their natural importance. Past their stylish allure and social imagery, the hazes assume a urgent part in supporting the fragile equilibrium of the

Good country environment. As they float through the glens, the fogs present their nurturing dampness to the vegetation, guaranteeing the essentialness of the regular world. Along these lines, the Murmuring Hazes become narrators of the past as well as watchmen of the land's continuous story.

As first light methodologies by and by, the Murmuring Hazes go through a change. The fogs scatter like slippery ghosts, uncovering the scene in the entirety of its crude excellence. The slopes, lochs, and standing stones rise out of the ethereal hug, as though waking from a dreamscape. The air, presently fresh and clear, conveys the buildup of the night's charm — a waiting wizardry that waits in the memory of the people who have submerged themselves in the persona of Scottish fogs.

To drench oneself into the persona of Scottish fogs is to set out on a significant excursion — an excursion through time, nature, and the actual soul of a land wealthy in history and legend. The Murmuring Hazes, with their consistently evolving dance, uncover a Scotland that rises above the limits of the conventional. They are narrators, craftsmen, and watchmen, winding around an embroidery that ties the past, present, and future into a consistent continuum. In the hug of these ethereal cover, one finds the excellence of the Good country scene as well as an association with something immortal and extraordinary — an association that waits, similar to the murmurs of the fogs, in the profundities of memory and creative mind.

1.2 Tales of ancient castles, lochs, and Highland landscapes veiled in fog.

Stories of Old Palaces, Lochs, and High country Scenes Hidden in Haze: A Story Excursion through Scotland's Supernatural Past

In the core of Scotland, where time appears to move at its own relaxed speed, stories of antiquated palaces, tranquil lochs, and High country scenes hidden in haze wake up like murmurs from hundreds of years past. The actual notice of these components summons a distinctive symbolism of a land saturated with history, where legends entwine with the real world, and the ethereal magnificence of nature unfurls in a spiritualist hit the dance floor with the fogs.

Consider, briefly, the outline of an old palace standing sentinel against the foggy setting of the High countries. These building wonders, demonstrating the veracity of hundreds of years of turbulent history, rise out of the haze as though monitored by ethereal sentinels. The murmurs of past times appear to stick to the stones, telling stories of gallantry, fights, and the strength of the people who called these fortifications home.

One such famous construction is the Eilean Donan Palace, arranged at the juncture of three lochs — Duich, Alsh, and Long. As the fogs envelop this archaic magnum opus, the palace shows up as though suspended between the sky and the earth. Its endured walls, kissed by the soddenness of the haze, become materials that bear the signs of time and history. Each stone appears to hold inside it the reverberations of the tribes, heroes, and darlings whose accounts are woven into the actual texture of the palace's presence.

Past Eilean Donan, the actual scene turns into a person in the fantastic story of Scottish fog hidden stories. The glens, with their undulating territory and lavish plant life, take on a supernatural quality when embraced by the ethereal fogs. It is as though the actual soul of the land arises through the haze, making a dreamscape that obscures the limits between the substantial and the fantastical.

The fogs, emerging from the lochs and wandering through the glens, have the ability to change the conventional into the unprecedented. Forests, rich with old trees and tangled foliage, become charmed domains where legendary animals could track down asylum. It is in these fog loaded woods that the creative mind takes off, imagining an existence where the limits of the truth are mellowed by the rings of haze.

In the legend of Scottish High countries, the lochs assume a focal part as the two observers and managers of the stories that unfurl around their shores. Loch Ness, famous for the slippery animal said to occupy its profundities, takes on an additional layer of secret when embraced by the moving fogs. The dim waters appear to hold privileged insights that the haze just alludes to, making an environment of both fear and interest.

As sunrise breaks over the lochs, the fogs rise like an ethereal expressive dance, uncovering and disguising in an entrancing musicality. The play of light on water, separated through the fog, changes the scene into a scene that reflects the glorious excellence of a fantasy. Lochs become intelligent mirrors, catching the pith of the encompassing scenes and projecting them into a domain where reality and deception interlace.

The interaction among lochs and fogs isn't restricted to Loch Ness alone. Across the Scottish Good countries, from Loch Lomond to Loch Tay, the waters reflect the always changing temperaments of the sky. Maybe the lochs become channels between the natural domain and the divine, with the fogs filling in as the ethereal scaffold that interfaces the two. In this amicable dance of components, Scotland's normal excellence arrives at a crescendo that reverberates with the people who take the stand concerning the exhibition.

As one digs further into the stories of fog hidden scenes, the folklore of the High countries comes to the very front. The old Celts, who once possessed these grounds, wove many-sided stories of divinities, spirits, and mysterious creatures that tracked down comfort in the regular world.

The fogs, in these stories, turned into the actual sign of the cloak between the human domain and the Otherworld — where the ethereal and the substantial coincided.

Legends of the Cailleach, a supernatural figure related with winter and the evolving seasons, frequently portray her winding around the fogs as though making an embroidery that covers the land. Her presence is felt in the chill of the haze loaded air, and her impact stretches out to the actual patterns of nature.

In the core of winter, when the fogs are most predominant, the Cailleach's touch appears to wait, forming the scene into a domain where time is both frozen and liquid.

The Murmuring Hazes, as they are frequently called, act as courses for the spirits of the land. It is expressed that inside the foggy hug of the Good countries, one could get a brief look at the pixie society — tricky creatures that bounce between the shadows and the light. These mysterious elements, as per old stories, track down shelter in the folds of the haze, uncovering themselves just to those with a sharp eye and an open heart.

The antiquated confidence in "slim spots," where the cover between the human domain and the otherworldly is permeable, finds reverberation in the fog covered glens and lochs. There one could experience the pixie society or hear the frightful types of antiquated tunes conveyed by the breeze. In the tranquil isolation of these slender spots, the mysterious and the ordinary meet, making a feeling of marvel that rises above the regular.

The ethereal fogs, past their social and fanciful importance, assume a urgent part in molding the barometrical states of the High countries. The temperature differentials between the cool land and the air make the best circumstances for the development of the hazes. As soggy air ascends from lochs and waterways, it entwines with the cooler air above, bringing about the introduction of the baffling fogs that have become inseparable from the Scottish scene.

In the towns settled inside the folds of the High countries, local people respect the fogs with a mix of love and commonality. To them, the hazes are not just barometrical peculiarities but rather living elements with their very own feeling. Stories are gone down through ages — of customs performed at the edges of the fog, where the cloak between the seen and the inconspicuous is at its most slender. These customs, well established in custom, are a demonstration of the getting through association between individuals of Scotland and the otherworldly fogs that shape their scene.

The stories of Scottish fogs track down articulation in fables as well as in the rich abstract customs of the country. Essayists and artists, roused by the reminiscent magnificence of fog hidden scenes, have created stories that catch the substance of the Good countries. Sir Walter Scott, a scholarly monster of the Heartfelt time, wove the climatic components of Scotland into his works, making an abstract inheritance that keeps on reverberating with perusers today.

In contemporary writing, writers keep on drawing motivation from the fog loaded scenes of Scotland. Crafted by essayists like Neil Gaiman and Diana Gabaldon, with their fantastical components and time-traveling accounts, bring out the enchanted characteristics of the High countries. The fogs, in these scholarly manifestations, become illustrations for the liminal spaces where the past and the present converge.

Workmanship, as well, has been a strong mode for catching the charm of fog hidden scenes. Painters, from the Scottish Colourists to contemporary specialists, have looked to convey the air exchange among light and mist on material. The visual portrayal of fog covered palaces, lochs, and glens turns into a demonstration of the getting through interest with the ethereal excellence of the Scottish Good countries.

The impact of fog hidden scenes stretches out past writing and workmanship; it saturates the actual character of Scotland's social legacy. The unpleasant kinds of customary Scottish music, brought by the breeze through fog loaded glens, summon a feeling of wistfulness and yearning. The bagpipes, frequently connected with the Good countries, appear to reverberate with the soul of the actual land, their songs entwining with the murmurs of the fogs.

The stories of old palaces, lochs, and High country scenes hidden in haze are not just stories — they are a living story that unfurls with each foggy hug. Scotland, with its rich history and otherworldly charm, welcomes the individuals who adventure into its fog loaded domains to turn out to be essential for a bigger embroidery. The fogs, as ethereal narrators, weave a story that rises above time and welcomes the inquisitive explorer to drench themselves in this present reality where reality and dream meet in a dance of fog and memory. In the core of the Scottish Good countries, the foggy scenes become a setting as well as a necessary piece of the story — a steadily changing material whereupon the tales of the past, present, and future are painted in the delicate tones of the ethereal fogs.

1.3 Unraveling the folklore and legends tied to the misty moors.

Unwinding the Fables and Legends Attached to the Dim Fields: A Profound Plunge into the Secrets of the High countries

As the morning sun graces the far reaching fields of the Scottish High countries, a dreamlike scene unfurls — the foggy fields wake up with an ethereal dance, covered in legends and fables that reverberation through the ages. These fog loaded scenes, with their unpleasant magnificence and cryptic environment, have been the material for endless stories turned by the oral customs of the Good country individuals. To unwind the fables and legends attached to the hazy fields is to set out on an excursion into the actual heart of Scotland's social legacy, where the common becomes uncommon and the cloak between the seen and the concealed is at its most slender.

The fields, tremendous territories of open land described by heather-covered slopes and wandering streams, act as the scenery for probably the most persevering through fantasies and legends in Scottish fables. In the hug of the fog, the fields take on a powerful quality, turning into a domain where reality and dream combine. It is inside this climatic woven artwork that the stories of antiquated legends, powerful creatures, and magical events track down rich ground.

One can't dive into the cloudy fields without experiencing the pervasive figure of the High country champion — a focal prime example in the legends of Scotland. These champions, frequently portrayed as furious and respectable, rise out of the fogs like ghosts of a former time. Their stories are woven into the actual texture of the fields, where fights were battled, and families had a special interest in the land. The fogs, in these stories, become a similitude for the progression of time, darkening the subtleties of history and leaving just reverberates of the fighter soul that once wandered the slopes.

One such unbelievable figure is the spooky nebulous vision of a Good country hero known as the "Green Woman of Balnain." As per neighborhood old stories, this otherworldly lady, hung in a green plaid, torment the fields close to Loch Ness. As the fog plunges upon the scene, the Green Woman is said to show up, meandering the slopes looking for her lost love. Her story, in the same way as other others, entwines love, misfortune, and the getting through association between the Good country individuals and their enchanted environmental factors.

The hazy fields likewise play host to a bunch of extraordinary creatures, each with own arrangement of stories have been gone down through ages. Among these substances is the "Each Uisge," a water horse that is said to possess the lochs and streams of the High countries. Shrouded in fog, the Each Uisge is accepted to draw clueless explorers into its watery space, just to uncover its valid, malignant nature. The stories of such animals, brought into the world from the foggy scenes, act as preventative tokens of the inconspicuous risks that might anticipate the individuals who adventure excessively far into the fields.

In the panthcon of Scottish legends, the fields are likewise home to the "Bean Nighe," an unearthly washerwoman who is said to predict the passings of the people who cross her way. Hung in a green cover and frequently spotted close to waterways, the Bean Nighe is a sign of looming destruction. Her presence in the dim fields adds a component of extraordinary premonition, where the limit between the residing and the ghostly is obscured by the whirling haze.

The hazy fields act as the stage for a huge number of stories including the "Cailleach," a legendary witch related with winter and the evolving seasons. In Celtic folklore, the Cailleach is said to shape the scene with her strong sledge, and her presence is felt especially during the colder months when the fields are many times hidden in ice and fog. Her impact isn't just apparent in the actual components of the fields yet in addition in the immaterial soul of the land, where the progression of time is set apart by the changing tones of the fog.

Among the most notable animals in Scottish legends are the pixies, frequently connected with the fields and their hazy spans. These tricky creatures, known as the "Daoine Sìth," are said to possess the secret corners of the scene, uncovering themselves just to those with a sharp eye and a good nature.

The fog, in these stories, turns into an otherworldly shroud that covers the doors to pixie domains, where time streams distinctively and the conventional principles of the truth are suspended.

The stories of pixie experiences in the fields frequently include people who, tricked by the charming music of the pixie society, wind up shipped to a domain past the fog. Such experiences are set apart by a feeling of immortality, where a solitary night in the pixie domain might liken to years in the human world. These accounts, reverberating through the hazy fields, act as a demonstration of the persevering through confidence in the conjunction of the otherworldly and the regular.

The hazy fields additionally harbor legends of old stones and hallowed locales that give testimony regarding the otherworldly acts of the High country individuals. Standing stones, like those found at Clava Cairns, become central focuses for stories of custom and mystery. In the cloudy hug of sunrise or nightfall, the stones are said to wake up with energy, and the actual fields become a liminal space where the shroud between the physical and the otherworldly is at its most slender.

The ancient stone circles that spot the fields are frequently ascribed to the mysterious ability of druids and antiquated diviners. In the dim fields, these stone circles take on an emanation of veneration, as though the very earth underneath them holds the mysteries of the past. The old stories encompassing these old locales discusses services directed under the shroud of fog, where the limits between the natural and the heavenly were accepted to break up.

The dim fields, in their ability as both observer and stage, highlight unmistakably in the oral customs of anthems and tunes. These melodic stories, went down through ages, frequently retell the stories of adoration, misfortune, and courage related with the Good country scene. The fog turns into a common theme in these sytheses, representing the vaporous idea of life and the transient magnificence of the fields.

In the ditty of "Cap Lin," the foggy fields act as the setting for a story of adoration, charm, and recovery. The hero, Cap Lin, is caught by the Sovereign of the Pixies and bound to her administration. The fog, depicted as a "small, hazy field," turns into the edge between the human world and the pixie domain. The melody, sung by ages of narrators, changes the fog into an enchanted gateway that rises above the limits of the real world.

The hazy fields are additionally saturated with oceanic legends, especially along the tough shoreline of the Good countries. Stories of spooky boats arising out of the haze, monitored by apparition groups, add a component of sea persona to the area. The fogs, coming in from the ocean, become an otherworldly drapery that covers the marine legends in a demeanor of secret and despairing.

One such sea legend is that of the "Apparition Flautist of Clanyard Cove." As indicated by neighborhood fables, the spooky sound of bagpipes can be heard reverberating across the foggy waters of the straight. The wellspring of the unpleasant tune is accepted to be an otherworldly flute player, meandering the shores with his ghost canine. The fogs, in this story, act as both a visual and hear-able scenery to the powerful events attached to the waterfront scene.

The cloudy fields, past their relationship with old stories and legends, assume a urgent part in forming the environmental states of the High countries. The temperature differentials between the cool land and the air make the best circumstances for the arrangement of the hazes. As wet air ascends from lochs and waterways, it entwines with the cooler air above, bringing about the introduction of the baffling fogs that wrap the fields in their ghostly hug.

The biological meaning of the dim fields reaches out past their air excellence. The dampness loaded air conveyed by the fogs gives food to the verdure of the Good countries. Heather-covered slopes, antiquated trees, and overgrown lowlands flourish in the soggy circumstances made by the whirling fogs. Along these lines, the fog becomes a narrator of the past as well as a nurturing force that sustains the sensitive equilibrium of the environment.

As day goes to night on the dim fields, the scene goes through a change. The fogs, enlightened by the delicate sparkle of twilight, take on a practically strange glow. The air becomes accused of a feeling of charm, as though the actual texture of the truth is extended slender within the sight of these slippery cover. Dusk in the fields, with the fog shrouding the scene, is the point at which the conventional standards of the world appear to release their hold.

Unwinding the fables and legends attached to the foggy fields is to dig into the actual soul of Scotland — a land where fantasy and reality entwine in the fog loaded scenes. The fields, hidden in haze, become a material whereupon the stories of High country champions, otherworldly creatures, and old stones are painted in shades of secret and marvel. The fog, similar to a transient narrator, winds around stories that rise above time, welcoming the people who adventure into the fields to turn out to be essential for a bigger embroidery of fantasy and memory. In the core of the Scottish Good countries, the cloudy fields stay not just a demonstration of the getting through force of oral practices yet in addition a residing demonstration of the mysterious charm of a scene where the customary is changed into the uncommon by the twirling cloak of haze.

Chapter 2

Himalayan Heights
Mystical Blankets of Nepal

Nepal, a land where the sky contacts the earth at its most elevated tops, is enhanced with an ethereal delight that rises above the customary. Settled in the core of the Himalayas, this little yet captivating nation is covered in an always present mysterious cover — the twirling fogs that shroud the transcending tops and verdant valleys. The Himalayan levels of Nepal, with their snow-covered highest points and fog loaded scenes, summon a feeling of stunningness and miracle that is well established in the social, otherworldly, and normal embroidery of the locale.

The Himalayan reach, with eight of the world's fourteen most elevated tops, including the great Mount Everest, remains as a symbol of Nepal's geological loftiness. As the primary light of sunrise breaks over the transcending tops, a wonderful scene unfurls — the magical covers of fog start their climb, uncovering a scene that appears to have a place with the domains of dreams. This peculiarity, happening all through the year however most noticeably during the pre-rainstorm and post-storm seasons, has turned into a vital piece of Nepal's personality, molding its way of life, legends, and the actual quintessence of its being.

The cloudy scenes of Nepal are not restricted to a particular district; rather, they embrace the different geography of the country. From the high-height levels of Colt to the rich backwoods of the Annapurna and Langtang areas, the fogs wind through the land, making an always changing visual ensemble. In the swamps of Terai, where the Himalayas steadily give way to subtropical fields, the fog rises like a spooky cloak, changing the scene into a dreamscape where the limits between the unmistakable and the immaterial haze.

The beginnings of the fog in the Himalayan levels are profoundly entwined with the geological and meteorological complexities of the district. The crash of warm, sodden air from the Indian fields with the cool, dry air from the Tibetan level makes the best circumstances for the development of fogs. As the air rises along the mountain slants, it cools, and dampness gathers to shape the ethereal cloak that cover the pinnacles and valleys. This climatic dance, a sensitive exchange of temperature and height, is liable for the charming foggy scenes that enamor those lucky enough to observe them.

The Himalayan fogs are not only meteorological peculiarities; they are living substances that reinvigorate the stories of the land. In the social and profound customs of Nepal, the fogs are frequently thought to be sacrosanct, conveying with them a feeling of supernatural quality and heavenly presence. It is accepted that the whirling shroud of fog interface the earth to the sky, giving a course to divine energies to slip upon the consecrated scenes of the Himalayas.

In the folklore of Nepal, the fog loaded levels are related with the residence of the divine beings. The transcending tops, wreathed in fog, become flights of stairs to the sky where divinities live. Mountains like Machapuchare and Annapurna are accepted to abide spots of heavenly creatures, and the fogs that encompass them are viewed as cloak that different the human domain from the divine homes. This conviction framework, profoundly imbued in the social texture of Nepal, adds a layer of love to the foggy scenes, hoisting them from simple normal peculiarities to hallowed domains.

Perhaps of the most notable top in the cloudy hug of the Himalayas is Mount Machapuchare, frequently alluded to as the "Fish Tail" mountain. Its superb culmination, unendingly covered in fog, deserves it a spot in the topographical records as well as in the otherworldly and social cognizance of the Nepalese public. Nearby old stories recounts Machapuchare as a sacrosanct top, untouchable to moving, keeping in mind the heavenly substances accepted to dwell there. The fog that envelopes its transcending tower is viewed as a heavenly shroud, veiling the holy culmination from the human look.

In the consecrated town of Muktinath, arranged at an elevation of 3,800 meters, the foggy levels take on a journey commendable importance. Muktinath, signifying "spot of freedom," is a site respected by the two Hindus and Buddhists.

As pioneers climb to the sanctuary intricate, the hazy atmosphere adds an ethereal quality to their otherworldly excursion. The fogs, in this holy setting, are not only meteorological peculiarities but rather conductors for divine endowments, conveying with them the cleaning quintessence of the Himalayan levels.

The social meaning of the fogs in Nepal stretches out past strict settings to day to day existence. In the conventional slope towns, where terraced fields grip to the slants, the fogs become piece of the farming musicality. The cool dampness conveyed by the fogs supports the yields, making rich circumstances for the development of rice, grain, and different staples. The farming schedule of Nepal, firmly receptive to the storms and the fog loaded mornings, mirrors the harmonious connection between individuals and the regular components that shape their vocations.

The Himalayan levels, hung in fog, additionally give the scenery to celebrations and festivities that mark the social schedule of Nepal. The celebration of Dashain, the main Hindu celebration in the nation, corresponds with the post-storm season when the fogs start to disclose the mountains. The celebration, representing the triumph of good over evil, is commended with enthusiasm and bliss against the scenery of cloudy scenes. The fogs, in this unique situation, become a similitude for the repeating idea of life, where snapshots of lack of definition are trailed by the disclosure of clearness and light.

The cloudy scenes of Nepal act as the setting for a bunch of cultural stories and oral practices that have been gone down through ages. In these accounts, the fogs are much of the time embodied, assuming the jobs of generous spirits or naughty elements. Accounts of mountain gods, known as "Yul Lha," and watchman spirits, called "Sasquatch," have large amounts of the rich woven artwork of Nepalese old stories. The fogs, as narrators, become characters in these stories, forming the predeterminations of individuals who abide in the shadow of the Himalayan levels.

The Sasquatch, a legendary gorilla like animal trusted by some to possess the distant precipitous districts, is frequently connected with the fogs of the Himalayas. In the oral practices of the Sherpa and Tibetan people group, the Sasquatch is said to move subtly through the cloudy scenes, abandoning perplexing impressions in the snow. The subtle idea of the Sasquatch, combined with the cloudy environmental elements, adds a quality of secret to the fables encompassing this legendary animal.

The cloudy levels are likewise interwoven with the unbelievable stories of Master Rinpoche, the Indian holy person attributed with acquainting Buddhism with the district. As per legends, Master Rinpoche, otherwise called Padmasambhava, flew on the rear of a tigress to the hallowed site of Maratika Cavern in eastern Nepal.

The fogs, in these stories, are viewed as the heavenly pathways that worked with the holy person's excursion through the Himalayas. Maratika

Cavern, concealed in the midst of fog covered slopes, has since turned into a critical journey site for Buddhists.

The cloudy levels of Nepal become a material for creative articulation, motivating artists, essayists, and visual specialists to catch the slippery excellence of the scenes. The refrains of Nepali writers, like Lekhnath Paudyal and Laxmi Prasad Devkota, frequently summon the fog loaded mornings and the otherworldly reverberation of the Himalayan levels. Painters, as well, have looked to convey the barometrical interchange among light and fog on material, making show-stoppers that mirror the radiant magnificence of the Nepalese scene.

The impact of the cloudy levels reaches out past the social and creative domains to the domain of experience and investigation. Nepal, frequently alluded to as the "traveler's heaven," draws in swashbucklers from around the globe to set out on ventures into the core of the Himalayas. The journeying trails, for example, the Annapurna Circuit and the Everest Headquarters journey, offer unmatched chances to observe the cloudy scenes very close. For adventurers, the fogs become buddies on the path, making an always changing setting that adds a component of secret to their rocky odyssey.

The enchanted appeal of the Himalayan levels arrives at its apex in the Khumbu area, home to the world's most noteworthy pinnacle, Mount Everest. The trip to Everest Headquarters, a journey of sorts for mountain dwellers and lovers the same, takes on a dreamlike quality as the fogs wind through the valleys and high-elevation settlements. The customary Sherpa towns, with their request banners vacillating in the foggy breeze, become waypoints in an excursion that rises above the physical and wanders into the magical.

The Khumbu locale isn't just a door to Everest yet in addition a store of Sherpa culture and otherworldliness. The Tengboche Religious community, roosted on an edge in the midst of fog covered slopes, is a hallowed safe-haven where priests take part in ceremonies that reverberate with the profound energies of the Himalayas. The fog, thought about by the Sherpas as the breath of the mountains, turns into a medium through which petitions and mantras are conveyed to the heavenly domains.

As one climbs higher into the Himalayan levels, arriving at heights where oxygen levels are scant, the fog takes on a translucent quality. Chilly fogs, loaded down with ice precious stones, make a scene that looks like a divine wonderland. The request banners, decorated with mantras and shuddering in the frosty breeze, add sprinkles of variety to the monochromatic range of snow, fog, and rock. In this domain of limits, where the air is slender and the vistas extensive, the fogs become a demonstration of the unstoppable soul of the Himalayas.

The Himalayan levels of Nepal, with their cloudy shroud and transcending tops, are a visual exhibition as well as a living demonstration of the interconnectedness of nature, culture, and otherworldliness. The fogs, in their never-ending dance, become courses for the concealed powers that shape the land and the existences of the people who call it home. Nepal, with its dim levels, welcomes voyagers and searchers to drench themselves in a domain where the normal is changed into the unprecedented, and the cloak between the natural and the divine is lifted by the ethereal hug of the Himalayas.

2.1 Journeying to the mist-shrouded peaks of the Himalayas.

Traveling to the Fog Covered Pinnacles of the Himalayas: A Journey into the Core of Earth's Mightiest Mountains

In the records of human investigation and otherworldly mission, scarcely any scenes order the worship and appeal that the fog covered pinnacles of the Himalayas summon. This huge mountain range, frequently alluded to as the "House of Snow," ranges five nations, including India, Nepal, Bhutan, China, and Pakistan. Its transcending culminations, profound valleys, and ethereal fogs have coaxed swashbucklers, explorers, and searchers for quite a long time, bringing them into a domain where the natural and the heavenly merge. This story sets out on an excursion into the core of the Himalayas, investigating the persona of its fog covered tops and the significant effect they have had on human creative mind, otherworldliness, and the actual texture of neighborhood societies.

The Himalayas, shaped by the impact of the Indian and Eurasian structural plates, are a topographical wonder that stretches across 1,500 miles and envelops a shocking variety of scenes. This huge mountain range is home to a portion of the world's most elevated tops, including the notable Mount Everest, standing tall at 29,032 feet above ocean level. As one endeavors into the Himalayas, the scene changes from rich lower regions to transcending tops, each step uncovering another feature of the district's magnificence.

The excursion to the fog covered pinnacles of the Himalayas isn't simply an actual campaign however an otherworldly odyssey that rises above the limits of the commonplace. The appeal of the Himalayas lies in their sheer greatness as well as in the ethereal quality gave to them by the consistently present fogs. The fogs, ascending from the valleys and encompassing the pinnacles, make a supernatural climate that has enthralled the hearts and psyches of the individuals who try to wander into this hallowed domain.

The Himalayan fogs, frequently noticeable during explicit seasons, are a result of the complex meteorological and topographical elements of the district. As warm, wet air from the Indian fields crashes into the cool, dry air from the Tibetan level, the bulldup of dampness brings forth the whirling fogs that shroud the mountains. This meteorological dance, affected by the rainstorm and the high-elevation geology, shapes the dim scenes that have become inseparable from the Himalayan experience.

The excursion into the Himalayas starts with the rising through the lower regions, where terraced fields and interesting towns give a brief look into the agrarian and social existence of the district. The fogs, even at these lower elevations, loan an enchanted quality to the scene, veiling the valleys in a delicate hug. As one climbs further, abandoning the lower slopes and crossing through rhododendron woodlands, the fogs become partners on the path, making an always changing background that adds a component of secret to the excursion.

One of the famous entryways to the Himalayas is the Annapurna area in Nepal. The Annapurna Circuit, a journeying trail that circumnavigates the Annapurna Massif, takes travelers through a different scope of scenes, from subtropical woodlands to elevated glades. As the path climbs, the dim scenes unfurl, uncovering a reality where the limits between the natural and the heavenly appear to obscure. Towns like Ghorepani and Poon Slope, roosted on edges neglecting the valleys, become vantage focuses for seeing the groundbreaking excellence of the fogs as they dance through the mountains.

In the Annapurna Safe-haven, an icy bowl encompassed by transcending tops, the fogs take on an additional sensational and magical quality. As the principal light of day break washes the tops in a brilliant shine, the fogs start to rise, making a dreamlike vibe. The sheer walls of Annapurna and Machapuchare, hung in the ethereal shroud, become a material whereupon the play of light and fog unfurls. The safe-haven, tucked away in hazy charm, is a hallowed amphitheater where the loftiness of nature turns into a quiet orchestra.

The excursion into the core of the Himalayas frequently stretches out to the Langtang Valley, one more charming locale in Nepal. The Langtang journey takes travelers through rhododendron woods, curious towns, and high-elevation glades. The fogs, here as well, become necessary to the scene, making an environment that is both tranquil and tormenting. In the Kyanjin Gompa, a high-height settlement settled in the midst of the pinnacles, the fogs add a layer of greatness to the profound acts of the nearby devout local area. The request banners, decorated with mantras and vacillating in the cloudy breeze, become conductors for the yearnings of the people who look for comfort in the Himalayan levels.

As one excursions more profound into the Himalayas, the scene changes into a domain of high-elevation desert and rough territories. Horse, a district frequently alluded to as the "Place that is known for Lo," is a social and geological gold mine. The fogs, blending with the residue of the bone-dry scenes, make a true to life impact, projecting a powerful shade over the old cloisters and caverns that dab the locale. In places like Lo Manthang, the previous capital of the Realm of Colt, the fogs become worldly cloak that transport the onlooker to a former period where the reverberations of old societies resound through the breezes.

The Himalayas, past their actual gloriousness, are imbued with profound importance for assorted networks. For Hindus, the Himalayas are viewed as the habitation of the divine beings, and the fogs that wrap the pinnacles are viewed as heavenly articles of clothing that cover the heavenly domains. The hallowed waterway Ganges, starting from the Gangotri Ice sheet in the Himalayas, is accepted to slip from the sky, conveying with it the otherworldly virtue of the mountains. Journeys to the Roast Dham, which incorporate the holy destinations of Yamunotri, Gangotri, Kedarnath, and Badrinath, are embraced by millions looking for profound recovery in the midst of the fog covered tops.

The Hindu journey to Mount Kailash, thought about the natural dwelling place of Master Shiva, is a hallowed endeavor that includes circumambulating the sacred pinnacle. The fogs that encase Mount Kailash, arranged in the distant western Himalayas, add a demeanor of mystery to this otherworldly mission. The excursion to Kailash, through strenuous territories and high passes, turns into a trial of actual perseverance and otherworldly dedication. The fogs, ascending from the sacrosanct lakes and valleys, are viewed as favors gave by the heavenly to the individuals who track the way of journey.

Buddhism, with its profound roots in the Himalayan area, thinks about the mountains as hallowed archives of shrewdness and illumination. The fog covered tops, in Buddhist way of thinking, are representative of the cloak that cover the real essence of the real world. The act of circumambulating stupas and petitioning God wheels, frequently found along journeying courses, is accepted to create positive karma that is moved by the breezes and fogs, helping every single conscious being. In places like the Everest Headquarters journey, where Buddhist cloisters decorate the scene, the fogs become quiet observers to the cadenced serenades and customs that resound through the high-height domains.

The hazy scenes of the Himalayas additionally hold importance in Tibetan Buddhism, where consecrated locales are in many cases settled in distant valleys and high-elevation levels. The Yarlung Tsangpo Waterway, frequently alluded to as the "Brahmaputra" in India, has its source in the glacial masses of western Tibet. The fogs that ascent from the riverbanks and wander through the valleys are viewed as the breath of the mountains, conveying with them the embodiment of otherworldly lessons. The journey to Mount Kailash, a hallowed endeavor for the two Hindus and Buddhists, is saturated with the magical emanation of the Himalayan levels.

The fog covered pinnacles of the Himalayas are respected in strict settings as well as hold an extraordinary spot in the domain of reflection and profound thoughtfulness. The isolation and quietness of the mountains, combined with the steadily evolving fogs, establish a climate helpful for thought and self-disclosure. Yogis and experts of reflection have looked for the separation of the Himalayas for a very long time, withdrawing to caverns and isolations settled in the high-elevation domains. The fogs, veiling these singular homes, become gatekeepers of the significant experiences and acknowledge that searchers accomplish as they continued looking for higher awareness.

In the western Himalayas, the district of Himachal Pradesh in India is home to various old sanctuaries and cloisters, each with its own otherworldly reverberation. The cloudy scenes of spots like Dharamshala and McLeod Ganj, roosted on the lower regions of the Dhauladhar Reach, have drawn in profound pioneers and searchers from around the world. The lessons of Tibetan Buddhism, dispersed by His Heavenliness the Dalai Lama, have found a safe-haven in this fog covered sanctuary, where the reverberations of dharma resound through the valleys.

The excursion to the fog covered pinnacles of the Himalayas is likewise a journey for experience and investigation. Mountain dwellers, drawn by the test of overcoming the world's most elevated tops, have tried their fortitude against the considerable highest points of the Himalayan reach. The fogs, frequently viewed as the two partners and enemies, add a component of capriciousness to the mountaineering experience. As climbers rise through the differing elevations and microclimates, they experience the steadily changing temperaments of the mountains, from clear skies to thick covers of fog that dark the way forward.

The Annapurna and Everest districts, with their transcending pinnacles and specialized difficulties, have become notorious objections for mountain dwellers. The fog loaded mornings at high-height headquarters, like those at Annapurna and Everest, are snapshots of calm reflection for climbers planning to handle the considerable culminations. The fogs, rising and disseminating with the beat of the day, become quiet observers to the victories and afflictions of the people who try to wander into the flimsy quality of the Himalayan levels.

The Himalayan fogs, past their otherworldly and experience aspects, are urgent players in the natural equilibrium of the locale. The dampness loaded air conveyed by the fogs sustains the assorted verdure that call the Himalayas home. The elevated knolls, covered with an uproar of wildflowers, flourish in the cool and clammy circumstances made by the fogs. Uncommon and jeopardized species, for example, the snow panther and the red panda, find shelter in the remote and flawless scenes where the fogs assume an imperative part in supporting life.

The cloudy levels of the Himalayas likewise hold signs to the changing examples of environment and frosty elements. The retreat of ice sheets, noticeable in the diminishing ice covers and cold lakes, is an outcome of worldwide environmental change. The fogs, as vaporous as they might appear, convey the murmurs of natural changes that have expansive ramifications for the whole planet. Researchers and specialists, concentrating on the Himalayan biological systems, utilize the fogs as signs of air conditions and climatic movements that are reshaping the essence of the mountains.

The social legacy of the Himalayan people group is unpredictably woven into the fog covered scenes. The conventional engineering, with unpredictably cut wooden veneers and pagoda-style structures, mirrors the feel and craftsmanship of the neighborhood individuals.

Celebrations, set apart by bright parades and ceremonies, frequently happen against the scenery of dim pinnacles and valleys. The fogs, in these social festivals, become a representation for the temporariness of life and the repeating idea of presence.

The dim pinnacles of the Himalayas are not absent any trace of difficulties and dangers, both for the nearby networks and the voyagers who look to investigate this considerable landscape. Avalanches, torrential slides, and flighty weather patterns add a component of eccentricism to the cloudy scenes. Nearby people group, with their close information on the mountains, have fostered a cooperative relationship with the regular components. The fogs, in their impulsive dance, become the two sponsors and foes, shaping the lives and vocations of the people who dwell in the shadow of the Himalayan levels.

The excursion to the fog covered pinnacles of the Himalayas unfurls as a multi-layered investigation, enveloping the actual scenes as well as digging into the rich embroidery of fantasies, legends, and social stories that have been woven into the texture of this striking district.

As explorers rise higher into the Himalayan levels, the air becomes crisper, and the fogs take on a glasslike quality, changing the scene into a domain of ethereal excellence. The play of light and shadow on the snow-shrouded tops makes a visual display that challenges depiction. The cloudy shroud, presently touched with the shades of dawn or nightfall, add a dreamlike quality to the all encompassing vistas.

In the Khumbu district of Nepal, the Everest Headquarters journey is a journey for mountain dwellers and fans looking to be in the shadow of the world's most elevated top. The excursion to Everest is a steady submersion into the foggy levels, where petitioning heaven banners vacillate in the cold breeze, and the musical serenades of Buddhist religious communities resound through the valleys. The fogs, in this sacrosanct domain, are not simple meteorological peculiarities; they are transporters of otherworldly favors, entwining the normal and the heavenly in an amicable dance.

Mount Everest, known as Sagarmatha in Nepali and Chomolungma in Tibetan, is in excess of a topographical milestone; it is an image of human strength and the quest for the phenomenal. The fogs that wrap Everest become piece of its persona, covering the highest point in a demeanor of riddle. The climb to Everest, testing and risky, is an illustration for the human mission to rise above constraints and contact the heavenly.

The Sherpas, a native local area dwelling in the high-elevation districts of Nepal, are personally associated with the Himalayas. Their lives are laced with the fogs that shroud the mountains, and their social practices mirror a profound veneration for the normal components. The Sherpas, frequently filling in as guides and watchmen for travelers and climbers, explore the hazy paths with a significant comprehension of the mountains they call home.

In the Solu-Khumbu district, where the popular Tengboche Cloister is roosted on an edge, the fogs become channels for otherworldly energies. The religious community, encompassed by fog covered slopes, reverberates with the serenades of priests participated in customs that span the natural and the heavenly. The fogs, as the breath of the mountains, convey the requests of the people who look for comfort in the serenity of the Himalayan levels.

The Himalayan fogs likewise assume an essential part in forming the environments of the district. The dampness loaded air conveyed by the fogs supports a different scope of vegetation, making a fragile equilibrium that characterizes the biodiversity of the Himalayas. Uncommon orchids, snow capped rhododendrons, and restorative spices flourish in the cool and wet circumstances cultivated by the fogs. The subtle snow panther, adjusted to the high-elevation conditions, explores the hazy scenes with a tricky effortlessness, significant of the mysterious charm of the Himalayan levels.

As one endeavors into the antiquated realm of Bhutan, settled in the eastern Himalayas, the dim scenes keep on spellbinding the creative mind. Bhutan, frequently alluded to as the "Place that is known for the Thunder Mythical serpent," is a domain where customs and legends coincide with immaculate regular excellence. The cloisters, known as dzongs, roosted on slopes and precipices, become ethereal safe-havens where the fogs upgrade the otherworldly mood. The social acts of Bhutanese people group, saturated with Buddhist standards, stress the interconnectedness of every single living being — a way of thinking reflected in the dim hug of the mountains.

In the high-height levels of Tibet, the Himalayas assume an alternate personality. The hazy scenes, entwined with the tremendousness of the Tibetan Level, make a feeling of vast spread. The itinerant herders, who have navigated these levels for ages, live together as one with the cadence of the fogs. Their yaks, strong animals adjusted to the unforgiving circumstances, eat in foggy knolls, adding a hint of life to the eminent scenes.

Tibetan Buddhism, with its rich iconography and customs, tracks down articulation in the cloudy levels. Travelers circumambulate hallowed locales, like Mount Kailash and Lake Mansarovar, where the fogs become images of otherworldly sanitization and amazing quality. The Barkhor Road in Lhasa, enclosing the Jokhang Sanctuary, is a clamoring lane where lovers and dealers explore the hazy climate, making a lively embroidery of social trades.

In the western Himalayas of Pakistan, the Karakoram Reach rises grandly, decorated with a portion of the world's most elevated tops, including K2. The fogs, here, add a demeanor of secret to the remote scenes where glacial masses and transcending towers characterize the geography. The Karakoram Interstate, a demonstration of human designing in the midst of imposing territory, twists through fog loaded valleys, associating old civilizations and current desires.

As one digs into the social kaleidoscope of the Himalayas, the fables and legends implanted in the hazy scenes show some major signs of life. Legends of sasquatches, mountain gods, and legendary animals have large amounts of the oral practices of Himalayan people group. The fogs, with their always evolving structures, become the material whereupon these stories are painted, obscuring the lines among the real world and creative mind.

The stories of the sasquatch, an unbelievable gorilla like animal said to possess the far off precipitous districts, resound in the fog covered valleys. The puzzling impressions, ascribed to the sasquatch, become baffling engravings on the blanketed material of the Himalayas. The fogs, winding through old timberlands and disconnected gorges, convey with them the reverberations of these legendary experiences, welcoming swashbucklers to unwind the mysteries disguised in the core of the mountains.

The Himalayan levels are additionally decorated with hallowed lakes, each with its own legendary accounts. Lake Gosainkunda, settled in the Langtang district of Nepal, is viewed as a hallowed journey site. The fogs that drift over the unblemished waters are accepted to convey the endowments of Ruler Shiva. Explorers attempt challenging excursions to arrive at the cloudy shores, looking for profound restoration in the midst of the quietness of the lake.

As one plunges from the foggy levels, the excursion through the Himalayas turns into an intelligent reflection on the fleetingness, everything being equal. The fogs, vaporous and consistently changing, represent the transient idea of presence. The paths, cut by hundreds of years of strides, demonstrate the veracity of the progression of time, leaving engraves in the dim hallways of the mountains.

In the lower spans of the Himalayas, where the cloudy scenes change into subtropical woodlands and terraced fields, the social energy of the area comes to the front. Slope towns, with their conventional engineering and earthenware rooftops, offer a brief look into the day to day routines of networks formed by the hazy hug of the mountains. The fog, dropping into the valleys, turns into a delicate indication of the repetitive rhythms of life and the interconnectedness of every single living being.

The excursion to the fog covered pinnacles of the Himalayas rises above the limits of geology, culture, and otherworldliness. An odyssey coaxes voyagers to submerge themselves in the always evolving scenes, where the fogs become narrators, channels of old insight, and quiet observers to the bunch stories woven into the texture of the mountains. The Himalayan levels, with their dim cover and transcending highest points, welcome the individuals who adventure into their domains to turn out to be important for a bigger embroidery — a story molded by the interchange of nature, culture, and the unyielding soul of a locale that keeps on spellbinding the human spirit.

2.2 Exploring the spiritual and cultural significance of mist in Nepalese landscapes.

Investigating the Profound and Social Meaning of Fog in Nepalese Scenes

Nepal, a place that is known for stunning scenes and old customs, is enriched with an otherworldly wonder that rises above the conventional. Settled in the hug of the Himalayas, this little South Asian country is described by its assorted geology, going from the high-elevation levels of Horse to the lavish woods of the Annapurna and Langtang areas. One of the charming regular peculiarities that characterizes the Nepalese experience is the presence of fog, a sensitive cloak that covers the transcending pinnacles and valleys. In this investigation, we dig into the profound and social meaning of fog in Nepalese scenes, disentangling the strings of folklore, fables, and day to day existence that are joined with this ethereal peculiarity.

The Dance of Fog and Mountains:

The beginnings of fog in the Nepalese scenes are established in the perplexing dance among topography and meteorology. The impact of warm, clammy air from the Indian fields with the cool, dry air from the Tibetan level makes the best circumstances for the development of fog. As the rising air cools along the slants of the Himalayas, dampness consolidates, bringing forth the sensitive cover that describe foggy scenes. This environmental expressive dance isn't only a meteorological event; a movement shapes the actual embodiment of the Nepalese landscape.

The fog, rising and plunging with the rhythms of the seasons, turns into a living element that reinvigorates the scenes. In the early hours of the morning, as the primary light breaks over the spiked pinnacles, the fog starts its climb. Valleys stir to a world shrouded in a delicate cloudiness, where the limits between the unmistakable and the immaterial haze. The mountains, wreathed in fog, take on an extraordinary quality, welcoming consideration and respect.

Sacrosanct Levels:

In the profound practices of Nepal, the fog loaded scenes are not seen as simple atmospheric conditions; they are viewed as sacrosanct domains where the natural and the heavenly meet. The transcending pinnacles of the Himalayas, enclosed by the ethereal shroud of fog, are accepted to be dwelling places of divine beings and goddesses. Mountains like Machapuchare and Annapurna are viewed as residences of gods, and the fog that encompasses them is viewed as a divine shroud, veiling the consecrated culminations from mortal look.

The town of Muktinath, arranged at an elevation of 3,800 meters, represents the sacrosanct levels of Nepal. Muktinath, signifying "spot of freedom," is respected by the two Hindus and Buddhists. As travelers climb to the sanctuary intricate, the cloudy mood adds an ethereal quality to their otherworldly excursion. The fogs, in this hallowed setting, become more than meteorological peculiarities; they are viewed as courses for divine endowments, conveying the refining pith of the Himalayan levels.

The cloudy scenes likewise assume a vital part in the conventional acts of Tibetan Buddhism, which has profoundly impacted the otherworldly texture of Nepal. The rippling petitioning heaven banners, embellished with hallowed mantras, become noticeable through the fog, making a visual orchestra of commitment. Religious communities, roosted on edges and bluffs, become safe-havens where priests participate in ceremonies that reverberate with the profound energies of the mountains. The fogs, considered the breath of the mountains, become mediums through which petitions to God are conveyed to the heavenly domains.

Fables and Legends:

The foggy levels of Nepal are not quiet; they murmur stories of old fables and legends that have been gone down through ages. In these accounts, the fog is embodied, assuming the jobs of generous spirits or devilish elements. Accounts of mountain divinities, known as "Yul Lha," and gatekeeper spirits, called "Sasquatch," have large amounts of the rich embroidery of Nepalese old stories. The fogs, as narrators, become characters in these stories, molding the fates of individuals who stay in the shadow of the Himalayan levels.

The Sasquatch, a legendary chimp like animal trusted by some to possess the far off sloping districts, is frequently connected with the fogs of the Himalayas. In the oral practices of the Sherpa and Tibetan people group, the Sasquatch is said to move covertly through the hazy scenes, abandoning mysterious impressions in the snow. The subtle idea of the Sasquatch, combined with the foggy environmental elements, adds a demeanor of secret to the legends encompassing this legendary animal.

The foggy levels are likewise interwoven with the unbelievable stories of Master Rinpoche, the Indian holy person attributed with acquainting Buddhism with the locale. As per old stories, Master Rinpoche, otherwise called Padmasambhava, flew on the rear of a tigress to the sacrosanct site of Maratika Cavern in eastern Nepal. The fogs, in these accounts, are viewed as the divine pathways that worked with the holy person's excursion through the Himalayas. Maratika Cavern, concealed in the midst of fog covered slopes, has since turned into a huge journey site for Buddhists.

Social Reverberation:

The social meaning of fog in Nepal stretches out past strict settings to daily existence. In the customary slope towns, where terraced fields stick to the slants, the fogs become piece of the farming musicality. The cool dampness conveyed by the fogs supports the yields, making fruitful circumstances for the development of rice, grain, and different staples. The agrarian schedule of Nepal, firmly receptive to the storms and the fog loaded mornings, mirrors the cooperative connection between individuals and the normal components that shape their occupations.

The celebrations and festivities that mark the social schedule of Nepal frequently unfurl against the dim background of the Himalayan levels. Dashain, the main Hindu celebration in the nation, harmonizes with the post-storm season when the fogs start to reveal the mountains. The celebration, representing the triumph of good over evil, is commended with intensity and euphoria against the hazy scenes. The fogs, in this unique situation, become a representation for the recurrent idea of life, where difficulties are trailed by breakthrough moments and disclosure.

The cloudy scenes of Nepal become a material for creative articulation, motivating artists, essayists, and visual specialists to catch the tricky excellence of the scenes. The stanzas of Nepali writers, like Lekhnath Paudyal and Laxmi Prasad Devkota, frequently inspire the fog loaded mornings and the otherworldly reverberation of the Himalayan levels. Painters, as well, have looked to convey the air transaction among light and fog on material, making magnum opuses that mirror the grand excellence of the Nepalese scene.

Experience and Investigation:

The impact of the dim levels stretches out past the social and creative domains to the domain of experience and investigation. Nepal, frequently alluded to as the "traveler's heaven," draws in swashbucklers from around the globe to set out on ventures into the core of the Himalayas. The journeying trails, for example, the Annapurna Circuit and the Everest Headquarters journey, offer unrivaled chances to observe the cloudy scenes very close. For travelers, the fogs become partners on the path, making a steadily changing setting that adds a component of secret to their rugged odyssey.

The mysterious appeal of the Himalayan levels arrives at its apex in the Khumbu area, home to the world's most elevated top, Mount Everest. The trip to Everest Headquarters, a journey of sorts for mountain climbers and devotees the same, takes on a dreamlike quality as the fogs wind through the valleys and high-height settlements. The customary Sherpa towns, with their request banners rippling in the hazy breeze, become waypoints in an excursion that rises above the physical and wanders into the magical.

The Khumbu district isn't just an entryway to Everest yet additionally a store of Sherpa culture and otherworldliness. The Tengboche Cloister, roosted on an edge in the midst of fog covered slopes, is a consecrated safe-haven where priests participate in customs that reverberate with the otherworldly energies of the Himalayas. The fog, thought about by the Sherpas as the breath of the mountains, turns into a medium through which petitions and mantras are conveyed to the heavenly domains.

As one climbs higher into the Himalayan levels, arriving at heights where oxygen levels are scant, the fog takes on a glasslike quality. Cold fogs, weighed down with ice gems, make a scene that looks like a divine wonderland.

The request banners, embellished with mantras and vacillating in the frigid breeze, add sprinkles of variety to the monochromatic range of snow, fog, and rock. In this domain of limits, where the air is slim and the vistas far reaching, the fogs become a demonstration of the unyielding soul of the Himalayas.

The hazy levels of Nepal, with their interlaced otherworldly, social, and regular aspects, stand as a demonstration of the significant interconnectedness of mankind and the climate. The fogs, in their unending dance, become channels for the concealed powers that shape the land and the existences of the people who call it home. Nepal, with its dim levels, welcomes explorers and searchers to submerge themselves in a domain where the common is changed into the phenomenal, and the cloak between the natural and the divine is lifted by the ethereal hug of the Himalayas.

In the core of the Nepalese scenes, the fog turns out to be in excess of a meteorological peculiarity; it turns into a scaffold between the substantial and the extraordinary. The transcending tops, concealed in fog, become passages to domains where divine beings and legends live. The fog loaded valleys, with their terraced fields and old towns, reverberation with the social rhythms of a strong group. The fogs, in their quiet persuasiveness, convey the tales of Nepal — accounts of otherworldliness, experience, and regular daily existence — welcoming the people who adventure into their middle to turn out to be important for a story that rises above reality

2.3 Personal narratives of treks through clouds in the world's highest mountains.

Individual Accounts of Journeys Across Mists On the planet's Most noteworthy Mountains

Leaving on a trip across the world's most noteworthy mountains is an extraordinary excursion that rises above the domains of the physical and wanders into the heavenly. The transcending tops, frequently concealed in spiritualist mists, become both a test and a greeting — a challenge to unwind the mysteries hidden by the ethereal fogs. In this investigation, we dig into individual accounts of journeys across mists in probably the most striking mountain ranges on The planet, following the strides of travelers who thought for even a second to rise to the glorious culminations that touch the sky.

The Annapurna Circuit: An Ensemble of Mists and Valleys

The Annapurna Circuit, a traveling course enclosing the Annapurna Massif in the Himalayas of Nepal, is an excursion through scenes where mists and mountains take part in an unending dance. My experience on the Annapurna Circuit started in the energetic city of Pokhara, where the serrated pinnacles of the Annapurna Reach lingered not too far off, to some extent darkened by floating mists. The expectation was unmistakable as our traveling bunch set out, directed by the musical sound of our strides and the far off reverberations of streaming waterways.

Rising through terraced fields embellished with petitioning heaven hails, the foggy mornings turned into a necessary piece of our excursion. As we wandered higher into the Himalayan lower regions, the mists started to wind through the valleys, making a steadily changing embroidery of light and shadow. Each step carried us nearer to the core of the Annapurna Massif, and the mists, instead of impeding the view, added a component of secret to the scene.

One of the features of the Annapurna Circuit is the climb to Poon Slope, a vantage point that offers an all encompassing perspective on the encompassing pinnacles, including Annapurna and Dhaulagiri. The pre-dawn journey to Poon Slope unfurled in close to obscurity, directed exclusively by the flashing light emissions headlamps. As we arrived at the culmination, roosted over the mists, the principal light of sunrise painted the tops in tints of pink and gold. The mists, far beneath us, looked like an ocean of cotton, and the world appeared to stir from a fantasy.

The journey went on through rhododendron backwoods, where the fog gripped to the greenery covered trees, making a captivated feeling. Towns, like Ghorepani, showed up as though suspended in the mists, their conventional houses arising and vanishing with each passing hazy breeze. The cordiality of the nearby networks, their lives unpredictably associated with the rhythmic movement of the cloudy scenes, added profundity to the story of our excursion.

As we crossed the high-elevation deserts of Horse, the mists assumed an alternate personality. The bone-dry scenes, touched with red and ochre shades, appeared differently in relation to the cool fog that plummeted from the Tibetan level. The old cloisters of Lo Manthang, their white-washed walls enhanced with petitioning God banners, remained as quiet observers to the transaction between the magical mists and the rough territories. The Colt district, taken cover behind the downpour shadows of the Himalayas, unfurled as a domain where the mists conveyed murmurs of old societies and untold stories.

The Everest Headquarters Trip: In the midst of Mists and Goliaths

Setting out on the Everest Headquarters journey is a journey to the world's most elevated top, Mount Everest, where the mists become side-kicks on the path to the top of the world. My excursion to Everest started in Lukla, a little airstrip settled in the midst of emerald slopes. All along, the presence of mists was substantial, projecting a cloak of expectation over the traveling bunch. The way, twisting through Sherpa towns and rhododendron woodlands, uncovered transient looks at the transcending tops, their culminations taken cover behind the moving mists.

The town of Namche Market, roosted on a terraced incline, rose up out of the fog like a Himalayan desert garden. As we adjusted to the high heights, the mists became steady friends, creating shaded areas over the mind boggling organization of stone houses and petitioning God wheels.

The Everest area, with its rough landscape and taking off goliaths, enticed us ahead through valleys where the mists appeared to blend with the actual quintessence of the mountains.

The climb to Tengboche Religious community, a profound safe-haven in the core of the Everest locale, unfurled in the midst of dim scenes that elevated the feeling of respect. The religious community, encompassed by rhododendron trees decorated with petitioning God banners, resounded with the serenades of priests took part in immortal ceremonies. The mists, floating through the uneven amphitheater, became vessels for profound energies that pervaded the dainty air.

As we journeyed higher, abandoning the timberline and entering the domain of snow capped knolls, the mists took on another force. Chilly fogs, loaded down with ice gems, arranged the scenes in shades of silver. The Khumbu Ice sheet, an enormous stream of ice moving from the slants of Everest, rose up out of the mists like a frozen behemoth. The excursion through the cold moraines, where the smash of rock underneath our boots blended with the inconspicuous murmurs of the mists, was a demonstration of the crude force of the Himalayas.

Arriving at Everest Headquarters, settled at the foot of the Khumbu Icefall, was a dreamlike perfection of the trip. The mists, whirling around the pinnacles, made an always moving scene that appeared to repeat the difficulties looked by mountain dwellers endeavoring to vanquish the world's most noteworthy highest point. The request banners, vacillating in the frosty breeze, conveyed with them the expectations and goals of the people who tried to arrive at the apex of human accomplishment.

The Inca Trail: Cloud Woods and Antiquated Remains

In the core of the Andes Mountains, the Inca Trail in Peru winds through cloud timberlands and old remnants, offering a brief look into the supernatural scenes that once characterized the Inca development. My journey on the Inca Trail started at Kilometer 82, where the Urubamba Stream streamed close by the path, covered in early morning fog. The vestiges of Llactapata, to some extent hid by mists, alluded to the archeological miracles that lay ahead.

Rising through cloud backwoods, where orchids stuck to greenery covered trees, the fog turned into a residing substance that revived the thick foliage. The path, cleared with old stones laid by the Inca engineers hundreds of years prior, drove us through a maze of bends and porches. Each step disclosed new vistas, where the mists embraced the encompassing pinnacles and valleys, making a fanciful air.

Dead Lady's Pass, the most noteworthy point on the Inca Trail, tested both body and soul. As we rose into the flimsy air, the fog hidden the way forward, adding a component of secret to the challenging excursion. The mists, twirling around the mountain passes, conveyed murmurs of the old developments that once flourished in these high-elevation domains. The plunge into the Pacaymayo Valley, where the fog gripped to the rich vegetation, offered a snapshot of break and reflection.

The archeological site of Winay Wayna, settled on a mountainside and to some degree concealed by mists, filled in as a preface to the loftiness of Machu Picchu. The fog, floating through the terraced destroys and stone designs, turned into a true to life scenery to the stories of the Inca public. The feeling of wonder developed as we moved toward the Sun Door, Inti Punku, where Machu Picchu unfurled before us like a lost city rising up out of the cover of time and mists.

The dim morning at Machu Picchu, as the principal light broke over the sacrosanct bastion, was a snapshot of unadulterated charm. The vestiges, washed in a brilliant shine, appeared to rise up out of the mists like a delusion. The mists, twirling around the notable pinnacles of Huayna Picchu, added a feeling of show to the old cityscape. Remaining in the midst of the remnants, the fog turned into an extension associating the present to the secrets of a former period.

The Karakoram Expressway: Cloudscapes of Northern Pakistan

In the remote scenes of Northern Pakistan, the Karakoram Expressway twists through a portion of the world's most elevated mountain ranges, making an excursion through cloudscapes that reverberation the greatness of the locale. My journey along the Karakoram Thruway started in Skardu, where the strong Indus Stream streamed in the midst of transcending tops. As we wandered toward the north, the mists plunged from the sky to embrace the rough scenes of the Karakoram Reach.

The climb to Pixie Knolls, a legendary level at the foundation of Nanga Parbat, unfurled through thick timberlands and high glades. The mists, playing find the stowaway with the titanic massif, made a climate of expectation. Nanga Parbat, known as the "Executioner Mountain," remained as a quiet sentinel, somewhat hidden by floating fogs. The trip to Pixie Knolls, in the midst of the orchestra of mists and the stirring of mountain winds, felt like an excursion to the edge of the world.

The Karakoram Thruway, as it wound its direction through valleys and along sharp precipices, uncovered looks at antiquated glacial masses and taking off tops. The mists, ever-present in the high-elevation domains, added a component of unconventionality to the excursion. As we moved toward the Hunza Valley, where the transcending towers of Ultar Sar and Ladyfinger Pinnacle penetrated the sky, the hazy scenes turned into a material painted with the tints of experience and investigation.

Hunza, a place that is known for high mountain passes and terraced fields, embraced us with its cloudy appeal. The old Baltit Post, roosted on a rough projection, rose up out of the mists like a middle age bastion. The Hunza Stream, twisting through the valley, conveyed with it the narratives of the antiquated Silk Street dealers who crossed these high-elevation domains. The mists, twirling around the pinnacles of Rakaposhi and Diran, added a quality of secret to the scenes that charmed the faculties.

As we journeyed towards Khunjerab Pass, the most noteworthy cleared global line crossing on the planet, the mists took on a frigid attitude. The foggy scenes changed into a colder time of year wonderland, where frozen lakes and snow-covered tops characterized the landscape. Khunjerab Pass, with its rippling banners denoting the line among Pakistan and China, remained in the midst of the mists as a demonstration of the getting through soul of human association across the world's most elevated scenes.

The Cordillera Blanca: Andean Tops in Peruvian Mists

In the core of the Peruvian Andes, the Cordillera Blanca brags a few the world's most noteworthy pinnacles, where travelers explore through fog covered valleys and icy lakes. My excursion in the Cordillera Blanca started in Huaraz, a clamoring town encompassed by transcending culminations. The St Nick Cruz Trip, an exemplary course in the district, enticed with commitments of flawless scenes embellished with glacial masses and turquoise lakes.

Climbing through the Quebrada St Nick Cruz, the mists turned into our dependable friends. The lavish plant life of the lower valleys, where the fog gripped to the leaves of quenual trees, progressed into rough scenes enhanced with high-elevation verdure. The mists, floating through the gorges and over the mountain passes, made an always changing display that uplifted the feeling of experience.

The Alpamayo Headquarters, settled underneath the notorious pyramid-molded pinnacle of Alpamayo, unfurled in the midst of a dreamscape of mists and stone towers. The fog, ascending from icy lakes and wandering through the valleys, added a quality of dreamlike magnificence to the rough territory. Alpamayo, thought about perhaps of the most lovely mountain on the planet, remained as a quiet observer to the complex transaction between the normal components and the vaporous mists.

As we crossed Punta Association, a high mountain ignore at 4,700 meters, the mists slid to welcome us with a chill in the air. The chilly lakes beneath, mirroring the encompassing pinnacles and the floating mists, made a mosaic of varieties that appeared to resist the impediments of height. The plummet into the Huaripampa Valley, where conventional Andean towns specked the scenes, uncovered a social embroidery interlaced with dim mountains.

Carrying on to the emerald waters of Laguna 69, settled underneath the monstrous walls of Pisco and Chacraraju, the mists added a bit of show to the elevated scenes. The icy cirques, etched by centuries of ice and wind, showed up as amphitheaters where the mists played out a quiet expressive dance. The turquoise waters of Laguna 69, a gem supported in the arms of the Cordillera Blanca, mirrored the greatness of the pinnacles and the transient excellence of the fogs.

Of normal excellence and high-elevation ponders. These individual stories typify the quintessence of traveling across mists, welcoming perusers to leave on a vicarious excursion through the foggy domains of a portion of the world's most notable mountain ranges.

In the Peruvian Andes, the Cordillera Blanca presents a scene where travelers explore through valleys and over mountain passes, all their means joined by the moving dance of mists. The Alpamayo Headquarters, settled underneath the great pyramid-formed pinnacle of Alpamayo, fills in as a safe-haven where the fogs ascend from frosty lakes and entwine with the stone towers. It is where the ethereal magnificence of nature meets with the superb engineering of the mountains, and the mists, a long way from being simple barometrical peculiarities, become imaginative colleagues in the excellent plan of the scene.

The St Nick Cruz Journey, twisting through Quebrada St Nick Cruz, exemplifies the Andean experience of traveling across mists. The lower valleys, covered in lavish plant life, witness the fog sticking to the leaves of quenual trees, making a charmed air. As adventurers rise through rough scenes decorated with high-height greenery, the mists become partners on the excursion, uncovering stowed away pinnacles and disclosing icy lakes. The St Nick Cruz Journey is an orchestra of regular components, where the mists contribute their tricky notes to the congruity of the Andean good countries.

Turning towards Northern Pakistan, the Karakoram Roadway disentangles a story of investigation through fog loaded scenes. The excursion to Pixie Glades, settled at the foundation of Nanga Parbat, unfurls through thick timberlands and elevated knolls where the mists play find the stowaway with the enormous massif. Nanga Parbat, the "Executioner Mountain," remains as a quiet sentinel to some extent hidden by floating fogs. Traveling across this district wants to dare to the edge of the world, where the fogs convey with them the untold accounts of old societies and the difficulties looked by the individuals who thought for even a moment to investigate these high-height domains.

Hunza, a place that is known for high mountain passes and terraced fields, uncovers its hazy appeal as travelers adventure further into the Karakoram Reach. The old Baltit Stronghold, roosted on a rough projection, rises out of the mists like a middle age bastion, a demonstration of the locale's rich history. The transcending towers of Rakaposhi and Diran puncture through the twirling fogs, making an emotional scene that enraptures the faculties. The mists, floating around these pinnacles, add a quality of secret to the scenes, welcoming travelers to turn out to be important for the story of experience and investigation.

Khunjerab Pass, the most noteworthy cleared global boundary crossing on the planet, remains as a guide in the hazy scenes of Northern Pakistan. Travelers moving toward this pass observer the mists taking on a frosty disposition as the cloudy scenes change into a colder time of year wonderland.

Frozen lakes and snow-covered tops reclassify the landscape, and Khunjerab Pass, set apart by vacillating banners, turns into an emblematic gathering point among Pakistan and China. The fog, in this specific situation, turns into an extension associating countries and societies across the world's most elevated scenes.

Getting back to the Andes, the Inca Trail in Peru unfurls a story of journeying across fog covered valleys and old vestiges. The excursion to Machu Picchu, the crown gem of Inca civilization, is a journey through cloud woods where orchids stick to greenery covered trees. The path, cleared with old stones, leads travelers through a maze of curves and porches, uncovering new vistas with each step. The mists, floating through gorges and over mountain passes, make a consistently changing display that increases the feeling of experience and expectation.

Dead Lady's Pass, the most elevated point on the Inca Trail, challenges travelers both genuinely and profoundly. As they climb into the slim air, the fog shroud the way forward, adding a component of secret to the laborious excursion. The plummet into the Pacaymayo Valley, where the fog grips to lavish vegetation, offers a snapshot of reprieve and reflection. The archeological site of Winay Wayna, somewhat concealed by mists, fills in as a preface to the loftiness of Machu Picchu, where the fogs become a realistic background to the stories of the Inca public.

The foggy morning at Machu Picchu, as the principal light breaks over the hallowed bastion, is a snapshot of unadulterated charm. The remains, washed in a brilliant gleam, appear to rise up out of the mists like a lost city arousing from sleep. The mists, twirling around the famous pinnacles of Huayna Picchu, add a feeling of show to the old cityscape. Remaining in the midst of the remnants, the fog turns into an extension interfacing the present to the secrets of a past time, welcoming travelers to step into the domains of history and creative mind.

The individual stories of trips across mists on the planet's most elevated mountains summon a feeling of marvel and worship for the superb scenes that have propelled swashbucklers for ages. From the Himalayas to the Andes, from the Karakoram Reach to the Peruvian high countries, these accounts illustrate the ethereal excellence that unfurls when mists and mountains take part in an immortal dance. Each journey turns into a special section in the bigger story of human investigation and association with the eminent powers of nature. The fogs, a long way from being simple meteorological peculiarities, become basic components in the orchestra of high-elevation undertakings, welcoming the people who leave on these excursions to turn out to be important for a bigger embroidery woven by the hands of mists and monsters.

Chapter 3

Amazonian Secrets
Misty Rainforests of Brazil

Amazonian Privileged insights: Hazy Rainforests of Brazil

Setting out on an excursion into the core of the Amazon rainforest is an endeavor into a universe of unrivaled biodiversity, old secrets, and fog loaded scenes. The Amazon, frequently alluded to as the "lungs of the Earth," ranges numerous nations, however it is in Brazil that the genuine mysteries of this tremendous and puzzling wild unfurl. This investigation digs into the foggy rainforests of Brazil, revealing the biological miracles, social extravagance, and the complex dance between the woodland and the fog that characterize this unrivaled area.

The Hidden Domain of the Amazon:

The Amazon rainforest, with its huge region of rich vegetation and wandering streams, is a demonstration of the surprising variety of life on The planet. Covering more than 60% of Brazil's domain, the Brazilian Amazon is a vault of regular fortunes that have been covered in fog for centuries. As one endeavors into its profundities, the sheer size of the rainforest becomes obvious, with transcending trees, complicated water organizations, and an orchestra of untamed life making a living embroidery that reaches out as may be obvious.

The fog, a steady friend in the Amazonian skies, adds an ethereal quality to the scenes. In the early morning, as the sun's beams enter the thick covering, the fog ascends from the timberland floor, making an extraordinary climate. This fog, referred to locally as "garoa," is in excess of a meteorological peculiarity; a living substance encloses the rainforest by a sensitive hug, veiling mysteries and welcoming those enter to turn out to be essential for a bigger, more significant story.

Biodiversity Revealed:

The Amazon rainforest is hailed as one of the most biodiverse puts on earth, home to an expected 390 billion individual trees addressing around 16,000 distinct species. This amazing cluster of vegetation is supplemented by a similarly assorted fauna, including panthers, macaws, capybaras, and incalculable bug species. The fog, with its groundbreaking touch, turns into a quiet accomplice in this many-sided dance of life.

One of the privileged insights the fog uncovers is the presence of incalculable restorative plants that have been involved by native networks for ages. These plants, concealed in the midst of the thick vegetation, add to the tremendous pharmacopeia of the rainforest. Customary Amazonian people group, like the native clans of the Yanomami and Kayapo, have bridled the mending properties of these plants, transforming the cloudy domains into normal drug stores that hold the keys to both physical and profound prosperity.

As the fog rises, it uncovered the many-sided snare of life that flourishes in the understory of the rainforest. Orchids, bromeliads, and greeneries, decorated with dewdrops, make an entrancing scene. The fog turns into a medium through which supplements are moved from the covering to the timberland floor, supporting the rich biodiversity that characterizes the Amazon. In this multifaceted equilibrium, the fog arises as a fundamental player, supporting the actual backbone of the rainforest.

Native Insight and Secrets of the Timberland:

The foggy rainforests of Brazil hold environmental mysteries as well as the old insight of native networks that have coincided with the Amazon for centuries. Native clans, like the Ashaninka, Kayapo, and Tikuna, have created personal connections with the rainforest, seeing it as an asset as well as a living element with its own soul and cognizance.

For these networks, the fog conveys profound importance, going about as a conductor between the noticeable and undetectable domains. Customs and services are in many cases directed in the hazy mornings, where shamans cooperative with the woodland spirits, looking for direction and recuperating. The fog turns into a cloak that isolates the material world from the otherworldly, and the individuals who explore this domain with deference and respect gain experiences into the secrets of the woodland.

The native people groups of the Amazon have developed a significant comprehension of the restorative properties of plants, a considerable lot of which stay concealed to the undeveloped eye. The fog, by uncovering the dew-kissed leaves and fragile blooms, fills in as an aide for customary healers, or "curanderos," as they continued looking for regular cures. This information, went down through ages, is a residing demonstration of the cooperative connection between the foggy rainforests and the native societies that call it home.

Riverine Secrets: The Amazon's Sea-going Heart:

The Amazon Bowl is confused by a perplexing organization of waterways, the most famous of which is the strong Amazon Stream itself. As the fog ascends over these streams, it uncovers a watery maze that is both backbone and territory for endless species. The gathering of stream and fog is an exhibition of consistent restoration, where the components unite to shape the biology of the locale.

The Amazon Stream, streaming for north of 4,000 miles, is a demonstration of the gigantic force of water in molding the scene. The fog, ascending from the stream's surface, turns into a dance collaborate with the ebbs and flows, making fleeting shroud that add a fanciful quality to the environmental factors. Riverine people group, like those along the Solimões and Negro waterways, have figured out how to explore this amphibian domain, depending on the streams for food and transportation.

One of the insider facts the hazy streams reveal is the yearly peculiarity known as the "pororoca." This tsunami happens when the Atlantic Sea tides crash into the active waterway ebbs and flows, making a strong wave that movements upstream. The fog, looming over the waterway like an unearthly drapery, heightens the show of this regular exhibition. The pororoca isn't only a presentation of regular powers however an indication of the interconnectedness of the Amazon with the more extensive planetary frameworks.

Dangers in the Fog: Preservation Difficulties in the Amazon:

While the foggy rainforests of Brazil radiate an air of agelessness, they are not resistant to the dangers presented by human exercises. Deforestation, driven by logging, farming, and foundation improvement, has created a shaded area over the Amazon, with huge regions of once-rich scenes giving method for clearing cut regions. The fog, when a steady friend, presently looms over the scars left by human mediation, a quiet observer to the changing essence of the rainforest.

One of the difficulties in the cloudy domains is the infringement of horticulture, especially steers farming and soy development. As the fog disseminates, it discloses immense spreads of deforested land, where biodiversity is supplanted by monocultures. The fragile harmony between the backwoods and the fog is upset, prompting changes in precipitation designs, loss of territory, and a decrease in generally speaking environmental flexibility.

Another danger prowling in the fog is the unlawful logging of valuable hardwoods, driven by worldwide interest for wood. The fog, when a defensive cloak, presently uncovered the ways cut by lumberjacks into the core of the rainforest. Trees that have represented hundreds of years, holding onto different environments, are felled, upsetting the delicate harmony that supports life in the Amazon. The fog, in this unique circumstance, turns into an impactful sign of the pressing requirement for protection and reasonable practices.

Environmental change, with its expansive effects on worldwide weather conditions, likewise creates a shaded area over the hazy rainforests. Changes in temperature and precipitation systems can modify the fragile harmony between the backwoods and the fog, possibly prompting more continuous and extreme dry seasons. The fog, when a dependable accomplice in supporting the rainforest, turns into a variable in a situation that is progressively impacted by human-prompted environmental change.

Protection Endeavors and Trust in the Fog:

In the midst of the difficulties, there are beams of trust that radiate through the hazy rainforests of Brazil. Preservation drives, drove by both legislative and non-administrative associations, are working resolutely to secure and reestablish the Amazon. Native people group, with their profound association with the land, are at the front of these endeavors, going about as watchmen of the timberland and promoters for feasible practices.

The fog, in this unique circumstance, turns into a representation for the strength of the rainforest. Similarly as it waits and reestablishes itself, the Amazon has the ability to recuperate and recover whenever allowed the opportunity. Reforestation projects, pointed toward reestablishing regions that have been cleared, are picking up speed. The fog, when observer to the scars of deforestation, may yet shroud the recuperating scenes in a green cover of rejuvenation.

Native drove preservation endeavors center around safeguarding the woodland as well as on imparting conventional information to the more extensive world. The fog turns into a course for understanding, where the interconnectedness of all life is perceived and celebrated. Drives that engage native networks, for example, supportable agroforestry and eco-tourism, are showing the way that the dim rainforests can accommodate both natural protection and human prosperity.

Worldwide joint efforts and mindfulness crusades are additionally vital in tending to the worldwide meaning of the Amazon. The fog, which knows no political limits, highlights the interconnected idea of ecological difficulties. Drives that include numerous partners, including legislatures, enterprises, and nearby networks, are fundamental in creating all encompassing arrangements that rise above lines and address the main drivers of deforestation and ecological debasement.

Social Woven artwork: The Fog as Motivation:

Past its natural and protection importance, the foggy rainforests of Brazil have roused a rich social embroidery. Specialists, scholars, and performers have drawn upon the persona of the Amazon to make works that catch the creative mind and convey the profound associations among humankind and nature.

In writing, the fog turns into a scholarly gadget representing the obscure and the enchanted. Brazilian creators, like Euclides da Cunha and Milton Hatoum, have woven accounts that summon the foggy scenes as settings for stories of investigation, change, and self-disclosure. The fog, with its veiling and disclosing characteristics, turns into a representation for the layers of history and secret implanted in the rainforest.

Visual craftsmen, as well, have been enraptured by the hazy charm of the Amazon. Works of art and photos frequently portray the interchange among light and fog, displaying the charming excellence of the rainforest. The fog turns into a range of quieted tones, where the energetic greens of the foliage and the rich browns of the dirt mix consistently, making a visual orchestra that reverberates with the spirit.

Performers, propelled by the rhythms of the rainforest and the murmurs of the fog, have made tunes that reverberation the normal rhythm of the Amazon. Native music, with its entrancing beats and tormenting tunes, catches the substance of the cloudy scenes. The fog, in this hearable domain, turns into a quiet director coordinating the harmonies of the rainforest and the tunes of human articulation.

Exploring the Secrets of the Fog:

The dim rainforests of Brazil, with their mysteries hidden and revealed by the ethereal hug of garoa, stay a domain of marvel and intricacy. Exploring this scene requires logical comprehension as well as a profound appreciation for the social, otherworldly, and natural aspects that unite in the core of the Amazon.

As the fog rises and disperses, it uncovers the complicated dance between living things, the interconnectedness of biological systems, and the fragile equilibrium that supports the Amazon. It uncovered the difficulties presented by human exercises and the pressing requirement for preservation endeavors that rise above borders and political divisions.

The fog, with its extraordinary characteristics, turns into a representation for trust and versatility. In the midst of the dangers and difficulties, there is trust that the foggy rainforests will persevere, recover, and keep on rousing ages to come. The insider facts of the Amazon, murmured through the fog, welcome humankind to perceive its job as stewards of the Earth and caretakers of the secrets that stay in the core of the world's biggest and most charming rainforest.

3.1 Venturing into the heart of the Amazon rainforest.

Wandering into the Core of the Amazon Rainforest

Setting out on an excursion into the core of the Amazon rainforest is a considering wandering into one of the planet's most perplexing and captivating environments. The Amazon, frequently alluded to as the "lungs of the Earth," is an immense spread of unrivaled biodiversity, including more than 60% of Brazil's region. This investigation dives into the diverse domains of the Amazon, where transcending trees, winding streams, and mysterious fogs make a residing embroidery that heartbeats with life, insider facts, and natural miracles.

A Shelter of Monsters: Transcending Trees and Biodiversity

The Amazon rainforest, with its transcending shelter of monsters, remains as a demonstration of the surprising variety of life on The planet. The huge biodiversity inside this lavish green field is a mother lode of biological miracles. Overshadowing 100 feet in level, the new layer of the rainforest shade is possessed by great hardwoods, including mahogany, rosewood, and kapok trees. This highest layer, contacted by daylight and kissed by the downpour, shapes the multifaceted trap of life that characterizes the Amazon.

Wandering underneath the overhang, one enters the understory — a domain overflowing with life. Here, thick vegetation, including greeneries, bushes, and epiphytes, seeks daylight in a steady battle for endurance. The understory is a safe house for heap plant and creature species, each assuming a one of a kind part in the fragile equilibrium of the rainforest biological system. The Amazon, with its unrivaled biodiversity, flaunts an expected 390 billion individual trees addressing around 16,000 distinct species.

Enchanted Fogs and Ethereal Cover: The Garoa of the Amazon

As sunrise breaks over the Amazon, a magical peculiarity known as "garoa" uncovers itself — a fine fog that ascents from the woodland floor, making an ethereal cover that covers the rainforest in a fragile hug. This peculiarity, in excess of a meteorological event, is a living element that covers the Amazon in a peaceful, extraordinary dance. The garoa, with its veiling and divulging characteristics, adds an extraordinary feel to the rainforest, making way for the day's unfurling secrets.

The fog, ascending from the streams, tidal ponds, and vegetation, isn't just a uninvolved barometrical component. It assumes a basic part in the nature of the Amazon. As it scatters, it discharges dampness very high, adding to the mugginess that is fundamental for the soundness of the rainforest. The garoa, with its stroking contact, turns into a medium through which life-supporting water cycles are sustained, sustaining the actual embodiment of the Amazon.

An Orchestra of Sounds: Untamed life in the Amazonian Ensemble

As one endeavors further into the core of the Amazon, the orchestra of sounds turns into a hypnotizing tune that resonates through the rainforest. The bedlam of bird calls, monkey prattle, and bug murmurs makes a hear-able scene that mirrors the liveliness of life. Macaws, with their energetic plumage, make sprinkles of variety against the green shelter as their calls reverberation through the fog loaded air. Howler monkeys, with their unmistakable thunders, contribute profound bass notes to the orchestra, while bugs add piercing quavers and tweets, making a layered sythesis that is both base and captivating.

The hints of the Amazon are not only irregular commotion but rather a language that conveys the imperativeness and interconnectedness of its biological systems. Birds, for example, toucans and parrots, assume a urgent part in seed dispersal as they traverse the rainforest, adding to the recovery of vegetation. The calls of howler monkeys serve as regional markers as well as for the purpose of correspondence inside gatherings. The humming of bugs, frequently covered by the thick vegetation, turns into a vital part in the multifaceted dance of fertilization.

Native Insight: Gatekeepers of the Woods

For centuries, native networks have flourished together as one with the Amazon, seeing it not simply as an asset but rather as a living substance with its own soul and cognizance. The rainforest, to these networks, isn't a product to be taken advantage of yet a hallowed space to be worshipped and safeguarded. Native clans, including the Yanomami, Kayapo, and Ashaninka, have developed a personal connection with the Amazon, living together as one with its cycles and seasons.

The fog, for native networks, conveys profound importance, going about as a course between the noticeable and imperceptible domains. Customs and services frequently occur in the foggy mornings, where shamans community with the woodland spirits, looking for direction and recuperating. The native people groups of the Amazon view themselves not as champions but rather as stewards of the land, entrusted with protecting the fragile equilibrium that supports life in the rainforest.

Customary information held by these networks stretches out past otherworldly practices to a profound comprehension of the restorative properties of plants. The fog, with its extraordinary touch, turns into an aide for conventional healers, or "curanderos," as they continued looking for normal cures. This information, went down through ages, is a residing demonstration of the harmonious connection between the foggy rainforests and the native societies that call it home.

Exploring the Streams: Waterways as Life savers

The Amazon Bowl is confounded by a many-sided organization of streams, the most notorious of which is the powerful Amazon Waterway itself.

These streams, looking like veins and conduits of the rainforest, structure helps that support the assorted environments inside the Amazon. The gathering of waterway and fog is a display of consistent restoration, where the components meet to shape the environment of the locale.

Exploring the Amazon's streams divulges a watery maze that is both soul and natural surroundings for innumerable species. Conventional riverine networks, like those along the Solimões and Negro streams, have figured out how to explore this oceanic domain, depending on the waterways for food and transportation. Wooden kayaks, quietly skimming through the fog loaded waters, associate networks and give admittance to the core of the rainforest.

One of the mysteries the dim streams disclose is the yearly peculiarity known as the "pororoca." This tsunami happens when the Atlantic Sea tides crash into the active waterway ebbs and flows, making a strong wave that movements upstream. The fog, looming over the waterway like a ghastly shade, heightens the show of this regular display. The pororoca isn't only a presentation of normal powers yet an indication of the interconnectedness of the Amazon with the more extensive planetary frameworks.

Preservation Difficulties: Dangers Sneaking in the Fog

While the Amazon rainforest oozes a quality of immortality, it isn't invulnerable to the dangers presented by human exercises. Deforestation, driven by logging, farming, and foundation improvement, creates a shaded area over the Amazon, with huge territories of once-rich scenes giving method for clearing cut regions. The fog, when a steady friend, presently looms over the scars left by human mediation, a quiet observer to the changing essence of the rainforest.

One of the difficulties in the cloudy domains is the infringement of horticulture, especially steers farming and soy development. As the fog disseminates, it discloses immense scopes of deforested land, where biodiversity is supplanted by monocultures. The fragile harmony between the backwoods and the fog is disturbed, prompting changes in precipitation designs, loss of natural surroundings, and a decrease in generally biological strength.

Another danger hiding in the fog is the unlawful logging of valuable hardwoods, driven by worldwide interest for wood. The fog, when a defensive cover, presently uncovered the ways cut by lumberjacks into the core of the rainforest. Trees that have represented hundreds of years, holding onto different biological systems, are felled, upsetting the delicate balance that supports life in the Amazon. The fog, in this unique circumstance, turns into a piercing sign of the pressing requirement for preservation and reasonable practices.

Environmental change, with its sweeping effects on worldwide weather conditions, likewise creates a shaded area over the cloudy rainforests. Changes in temperature and precipitation systems can modify the sensitive harmony between the woodland and the fog, possibly prompting more regular and serious dry spells.

The fog, when a dependable accomplice in supporting the rainforest, turns into a variable in a situation that is progressively impacted by human-prompted environmental change.

Protection Endeavors: Trust in the Fog

In the midst of the difficulties, there are beams of trust that radiate through the cloudy rainforests of the Amazon. Preservation drives, drove by both administrative and non-legislative associations, are working enthusiastically to secure and reestablish the Amazon. Native people group, with their profound association with the land, are at the very front of these endeavors, going about as gatekeepers of the woodland and backers for economical practices.

The fog, in this specific circumstance, turns into a similitude for the strength of the rainforest. Similarly as it waits and reestablishes itself, the Amazon has the ability to recuperate and recover whenever allowed the opportunity. Reforestation projects, pointed toward reestablishing regions that have been cleared, are picking up speed. The fog, when observer to the scars of deforestation, may yet shroud the recuperating scenes in a green cover of rejuvenation.

Native drove preservation endeavors center around safeguarding the woods as well as on offering conventional information to the more extensive world. The fog turns into a conductor for understanding, where the interconnectedness of all life is perceived and celebrated. Drives that enable native networks, for example, supportable agroforestry and eco-tourism, are showing the way that the hazy rainforests can accommodate both natural preservation and human prosperity.

Worldwide coordinated efforts and mindfulness crusades are additionally critical in tending to the worldwide meaning of the Amazon. The fog, which knows no political limits, highlights the interconnected idea of natural difficulties. Drives that include various partners, including state run administrations, enterprises, and nearby networks, are fundamental in creating comprehensive arrangements that rise above lines and address the underlying drivers of deforestation and ecological debasement.

Social Embroidered artwork: The Fog as Motivation

Past its biological and protection importance, the foggy rainforests of the Amazon have propelled a rich social embroidery. Craftsmen, scholars, and performers have drawn upon the persona of the Amazon to make works that catch the creative mind and convey the profound associations among mankind and nature.

In writing, the fog turns into a scholarly gadget representing the obscure and the otherworldly. Brazilian creators, like Euclides da Cunha and Milton Hatoum, have woven stories that summon the dim scenes as settings for stories of investigation, change, and self-revelation. The fog, with its veiling and divulging characteristics, turns into a similitude for the layers of history and secret implanted in the rainforest.

Visual specialists, as well, have been enamored by the cloudy appeal of the Amazon. Canvases and photos frequently portray the exchange among light and fog, displaying the charming magnificence of the rainforest. The fog turns into a range of quieted tones, where the dynamic greens of the foliage and the rich browns of the dirt mix consistently, making a visual orchestra that reverberates with the spirit.

Performers, propelled by the rhythms of the rainforest and the murmurs of the fog, have made songs that reverberation the normal rhythm of the Amazon. Native music, with its mesmerizing beats and tormenting tunes, catches the embodiment of the dim scenes. The fog, in this hearable domain, turns into a quiet director organizing the harmonies of the rainforest and the tunes of human articulation.

Exploring the Secrets of the Fog

Wandering into the core of the Amazon rainforest is an excursion of significant importance — one that rises above the limits of science, preservation, and culture. It is an excursion into a domain where fog loaded scenes cover and uncover the privileged insights of a no nonsense substance that is the Amazon.

As the fog rises and scatters, it uncovers the multifaceted dance between living things, the interconnectedness of biological systems, and the sensitive equilibrium that supports the Amazon. It uncovered the difficulties presented by human exercises and the earnest requirement for preservation endeavors that rise above borders and political divisions.

The fog, with its extraordinary characteristics, turns into a similitude for trust and strength. In the midst of the dangers and difficulties, there is trust that the dim rainforests will persevere, recover, and keep on rousing ages to come. The insider facts of the Amazon, murmured through the fog, welcome humankind to perceive its job as stewards of the Earth and caretakers of the secrets that stay in the core of the world's biggest and most charming rainforest.

3.2 Discovering how mist shapes the biodiversity and ecosystems of the region.

Finding How Fog Shapes the Biodiversity and Biological systems of the Locale

Wandering into fog loaded scenes discloses a reality where the ethereal bit of fog turns into an expert stone carver, forming the actual texture of biodiversity and biological systems. This investigation dives into the unpredictable dance among fog and nature, uncovering what this environmental peculiarity means for the sensitive equilibrium of life in different areas across the globe.

Enchanted Ensemble of Fog in the Amazon Rainforest:

Setting out on an excursion into the core of the Amazon rainforest is a tactile inundation into an enchanted orchestra where fog assumes a vital part. The Amazon, with its immense scope of transcending trees and unpredictable streams, is hidden in the first part of the day embrace of fog, privately known as "garoa." This fine fog ascends from the woodland floor, adding a layer of charm to the generally different and lively environment.

As the fog disperses, it discharges dampness up high, adding to the moistness that is fundamental for the wellbeing of the rainforest. The Amazon's unpredictable trap of life, comprising of more than 390 billion individual trees and around 16,000 distinct species, depends on this fragile equilibrium. The fog becomes a meteorological event as well as a living element that supports the biodiversity of the district.

The garoa, with its veiling and disclosing characteristics, turns into a narrator in the Amazon's environmental story. It uncovers the secret verdure that flourish in the understory, where thick vegetation seeks daylight. Orchids, greeneries, and epiphytes, enhanced with dewdrops, make a hypnotizing exhibition as the fog reveals their sensitive excellence. The Amazon, subsequently, turns into a residing material where fog goes about as the brushstroke that uncovers the perplexing subtleties of a huge and interconnected environment.

The Dance of Mists in the Scottish High countries:

In the Scottish Good countries, fog winds around its own dance, changing the rough scenes into ethereal domains. The fog, frequently covering old palaces, lochs, and heather-covered slopes, turns into a climatic painter that obscures the lines among the real world and fantasy. The Good countries, with their emotional geography, are significantly molded by the consistently present fog that shroud the scene in a shroud of secret.

Lochs, reflect like in quiet climate, become charmed gateways to a different universe when embraced by fog. The fog, ascending from the virus waters and floating through glens, adds a quality of old sorcery to the Scottish Good countries. As it covers the heather-clad fields, the fog uncovers the quiet impressions of red deer and the slippery developments of Good country natural life. The biological system, with its solid greenery, is unpredictably connected to the fog, adjusting to the air dance that characterizes life in these rough scenes.

In the High countries, fog isn't simply a meteorological event; it is a social and biological power. The fog turns out to be important for High country legends, where antiquated stories discuss kelpies and spirits that rise out of the shroud of mists. The fog, in this specific situation, shapes the actual climate as well as the narratives and customs went down through ages. It turns into an extension interfacing the unmistakable and immaterial parts of the locale's social and normal legacy.

The Hidden Pinnacles of the Himalayas: Persona of Nepal's Covers of Fog:

The Himalayan levels of Nepal are delegated with cloudy covers that wrap the great pinnacles and valleys. As one excursions into this remarkable district, the fog turns into a characterizing highlight, molding the scene and impacting the biodiversity of the world's most elevated mountains. From the transcending pinnacles of Everest to the distant valleys, fog in the Himalayas is both a visual display and a natural power.

In the Khumbu Valley, where the notorious Everest Headquarters journey unfurls, fog cover the rough territory, making a powerful climate. The mists, floating through profound valleys and over cold moraines, uncover and hide the scene in a steady transaction. The fog, loaded down with the embodiment of high-elevation environments, turns into a quiet storyteller of the difficulties looked by the two travelers and the strong greenery that call the Himalayas home.

The biodiversity of the Himalayas, adjusted to outrageous heights and unforgiving circumstances, is personally connected to the fog. Uncommon species, for example, the tricky snow panther and the Himalayan tahr explore the fog loaded scenes with a feeling of beauty and variation. Snow capped knolls, decorated with lively rhododendron blossoms, wake up as the fog uncovers the sensitive excellence concealed in the folds of the mountains. The Himalayan biological system, formed by fog and height, is a demonstration of nature's capacity to flourish notwithstanding misfortune.

Old stories and Haze in the Irish Open country:

In the verdant scenes of Ireland, fog takes on a legendary quality, entwining with old stories and forming the social personality of the open country. The Irish open country, with its moving slopes, old palaces, and wandering waterways, turns into a material where fog paints stories of legends and old spirits. As the haze come in from the Atlantic, it turns into a phantom presence that adds a quality of persona to the emerald isle.

In Irish old stories, fog is frequently connected with the "Tuatha Dé Danann," a legendary race of creatures who, as per legend, showed up in Ireland on a hazy day. The fog, in this unique circumstance, turns into a shroud that covers the otherworldly and mystical domains occupied by old creatures. The scenes, hung in haze, bring out a feeling of immortality, where the over a wide span of time converge in a dance arranged by the consistently present fog.

The biological effect of fog in Ireland is additionally significant, particularly in its impact on the country's famous peat marshes. These exceptional biological systems, portrayed by wet, acidic circumstances, are formed by the fog that covers the open country. Greeneries, heathers, and remarkable plant species flourish in the fog loaded climate, making environments for an assortment of natural life. The fog, with its impact on the waterlogged scenes, turns into a supporting power that supports Ireland's particular natural networks.

Perplexing Fogs Across the Peruvian Andes:

In the Peruvian Andes, fog assumes a focal part in forming the scenes of the Cordillera Blanca and then some. The Andean district, described by high-height biological systems and sensational mountain view, encounters fog as a unique power that impacts both the greenery of this tough territory. The Cordillera Blanca, with its glaciated pinnacles and profound valleys, is hidden in fog that adds to the exceptional excellence and natural intricacy of the Andes.

The St Nick Cruz Trip, a well known course in the Cordillera Blanca, exemplifies the Andean experience of traveling across mists. The lower valleys, decorated with quenual trees and lavish vegetation, witness the fog sticking to leaves and making a charmed mood. As adventurers rise to higher elevations, the fog divulges stowed away pinnacles and uncovers frosty lakes, offering looks at the different biological systems that exist in the shadow of the Andean monsters.

The high-elevation environments of the Andes, molded by fog and outrageous circumstances, harbor interesting species like the Andean condor and the vicuña. These variations to high-elevation life exhibit the mind boggling connection between fog, height, and biodiversity. As the fog disseminates, it uncovers the strength of life in the Andes, where high plants, solid warm blooded creatures, and superb birds flourish in a fragile equilibrium that is both formed and supported by the barometrical dance of mists.

Pacific Northwest's Seaside Woven artwork: Haze's Effect on Cascadian Biological systems:

Along the Pacific Northwest shore of North America, an alternate sign of fog becomes the dominant focal point as seaside haze. This marine layer, driven by the gathering of warm and cold air flows, makes a special environmental peculiarity that impacts the biological systems of the district. From the transcending timberlands of redwoods to the rough shores of Oregon, waterfront mist turns into a characterizing highlight that shapes the biodiversity and biological elements of the Cascadian scenes.

Redwood Public and State Parks, home to the absolute tallest trees on The planet, are many times encompassed in beach front haze that come in from the Pacific Sea. The fog, loaded down with dampness, adds to the water supply of the old redwoods, supporting these transcending goliaths that have represented hundreds of years. The beach front haze, in this specific situation, turns into a life saver for the redwood biological systems, giving a persistent wellspring of water in the generally dry mid year months.

The impact of seaside haze reaches out past the redwood backwoods to the different biological systems along the Cascadian coast. From tide pools overflowing with marine life to greenery hung calm rainforests, fog turns into a binding together power that interfaces unique natural surroundings. Seabirds, marine well evolved creatures, and seaside plants have adjusted to the ordinary inundation of haze, making a complicated trap of communications that characterize life along the Pacific Northwest's powerful and steadily evolving shore.

The Mediterranean's Hit the dance floor with Fog: A Basic Power in Southern Europe:

The Mediterranean district, with its different scenes and rich social history, encounters fog as a dynamic and basic power that shapes both the regular and human conditions. From the olive forests of Greece to the noteworthy scenes of Italy, fog turns into an imperative player in the natural embroidery of Southern Europe. The unpredictable dance among land and ocean, molded by fog, characterizes the district's biodiversity and impacts its social customs.

In the early morning hours, fog frequently covers the olive plantations that spot the Mediterranean scene. The fog, beginning from the ocean, wraps the forests and makes a barometrical scene. Olive trees, with their brilliant leaves, become ethereal figures in the fog loaded climate. The biological effect is significant, as the fog adds to the dampness levels fundamental for olive development, a foundation of Mediterranean farming.

The islands of the Mediterranean, encompassed by the hug of fog, harbor interesting environments that are both tough and delicate. From the rough precipices of Crete to the rich scenes of Corsica, fog turns into a nurturing force that supports different verdure. The environmental variety of the Mediterranean, molded by fog and the transaction of land and ocean, is reflected in the social legacy of the district, where fantasies, customs, and horticultural practices are characteristically connected to the natural dance of fog.

The Job of Fog in Cold Tundras: An Unobtrusive Impact in Unforgiving Environments:

In the Icy tundras, where cruel environments win and the scene is overwhelmed by immense regions of cold and ruined magnificence, fog assumes an unpretentious yet urgent part. The Icy, portrayed by low temperatures and a short developing season, encounters fog as a peculiarity that impacts the delicate environments of this northernmost district. From the tundra fields of The Frozen North to the fjords of Norway, fog turns into an extraordinary power that shapes the biodiversity of the Cold scenes.

During the short Cold summer, fog frequently covers the tundra, making an air impact that intensifies the isolation and serenity of the district. The fog, brought into the world from the collaboration of cold air and hotter water bodies, adds a layer of protection to the tundra environments. Cold verdure, adjusted to outrageous circumstances, use the dampness from fog to fuel their brief yet extraordinary development spray throughout the mid year months.

In the Cold, fog isn't just a meteorological peculiarity; it is a connector of components in a sensitive and tough dance. The fog loaded air, conveying dampness from the encompassing oceans, impacts the elements of permafrost, molding the actual underpinnings of Icy scenes. The unpretentious impact of fog becomes obvious in the perplexing variations of Cold untamed life, from the subtle musk bulls to the transitory examples of Icy birds, each figuring out how to flourish despite outrageous circumstances.

Revealing the Secrets of Fog Across the Globe:

Finding how fog shapes the biodiversity and environments of various districts offers a significant understanding into the interconnectedness of nature and climate. From the Amazon rainforest's mysterious orchestra to the Cold tundra's inconspicuous dance, fog arises as a groundbreaking power that the two cover and uncovers the insider facts of our planet's different scenes.

As we venture through fog loaded conditions, we witness the sensitive harmony between the substantial and elusive parts of nature. Fog turns into a conductor through which life adjusts, flourishes, and develops, impacting everything from the tallest trees to the littlest organic entities. It is a power that supports biological systems as well as shapes social personalities, rousing fantasies, stories, and customs that resound with the networks occupying fog hung scenes.

In unwinding the secrets of fog across the globe, we find that this air peculiarity is definitely in excess of a temporary meteorological occasion. An essential power associates seas to mountains, woodlands to deserts, and societies to their genealogical scenes. Fog turns into an image of strength, transformation, and the complicated dance of life on The planet, making a permanent imprint on the biodiversity and biological systems it encompasses.

3.3 Indigenous perspectives on the mystical qualities of Amazonian mist.

Native Points of view on the Enchanted Characteristics of Amazonian Fog

In the core of the Amazon rainforest, where the ensemble of nature plays in a charming rhythm, native networks hold significant points of view on the otherworldly characteristics of the fog that cloak their hereditary terrains. For these networks, fog isn't simply a meteorological event; it is a living substance, a profound power that winds through the texture of their societies, interfacing them to the rhythms of the rainforest in manners that rise above the limits of the unmistakable and the immaterial.

Fog as a Living Substance:

To the native people groups of the Amazon, fog is in excess of an assortment of water drops suspended in the air; it is a living substance with its own soul. Fog, known as "garoa" in Portuguese, typifies a power that is both seen and concealed, a sign of the rainforest's breath. For the Yawanawá, Ashaninka, and endless different clans, fog is the breath of the actual woods, a vivify being that supports the land in its delicate hug.

In the embroidery of native cosmology, fog is a profound power that associates the natural domain with the otherworldly aspects. It is accepted to be the vehicle through which the woods speaks with its occupants.

Shamans, loved as arbiters between the noticeable and undetectable, direct customs and services in the cloudy mornings, looking for direction from the spirits of the backwoods. The fog turns into a consecrated medium, a conductor for the trading of energies that support both the rainforest and its native overseers.

Profound Importance and Ceremonial Practices:

The fog loaded mornings in the Amazon are sacrosanct minutes for native networks. The Wachiperi public, settled in the Peruvian Amazon, accept that the fog conveys messages from their progenitors. As the fog floats through the transcending trees, it is remembered to bring murmurs of direction and admonitions from the spirits of the people who strolled the woods ways before them. In light of this otherworldly association, the Wachiperi take part in customs, recognizing the fog as a courier and go between in their relationship with the concealed domains.

Shamans, the otherworldly pioneers and healers of native networks, assume a focal part in deciphering the language of the fog. The Shipibo public, known for their mind boggling mathematical workmanship propelled by Ayahuasca dreams, believe fog to be a domain where the spirits convey. Ayahuasca functions led in the fog are accepted to improve the shaman's capacity to associate with the profound aspects, opening experiences that guide the local area in issues of recuperating, concordance, and equilibrium.

Exploring the Cover between Universes:

For native networks, fog fills in as a cover between the seen and concealed, the unmistakable and elusive. The Huni Kuin, otherwise called the Kaxinawá, consider fog to be an edge between universes — a liminal space where the regular and heavenly coincide. Fog loaded scenes are seen as gateways, where the limits between the natural and soul domains obscure, welcoming fellowship with the backwoods spirits.

As the fog rises and moves through the covering, it turns into a living drapery that isolates the everyday from the supernatural. Native accounts are rich with stories of spirits and creatures that rise out of the fog, watchmen of the woods who uncover themselves in these transient minutes. The fog, hence, isn't a snag however a facilitator, welcoming native people groups to explore the limits of presence and interface with the concealed powers that shape their cosmologies.

The Garoa's Mending Contact:

Past its profound aspects, fog is viewed as by native networks to have recuperating properties. The Katukina public, staying in the Brazilian Amazon, accept that the garoa has a mitigating contact, both truly and profoundly. The fog is viewed as a delicate healer, lightening infirmities and reestablishing harmony to the body and soul. Native mending rehearses frequently include communing with the fog, embracing its extraordinary characteristics for both physical and magical prosperity.

The Wixárika, or Huichol, individuals of Mexico, take part in journey excursions to consecrated mountains, looking for fellowship with the heavenly. Fog loaded scenes, saw as sacrosanct spaces, are basic to these journeys. The fog, in this unique situation, isn't just an actual component yet an otherworldly aide, driving the Wixárika on an extraordinary excursion where mending and edification anticipate.

Guardianship and Stewardship:

Native points of view on fog stretch out past the mysterious to the reasonable, including a profound feeling of guardianship and stewardship.

The fog, as the breath of the timberland, is complicatedly attached to the prosperity of the Amazon environment. Native people group consider themselves to be stewards of the hazy domains, depended with the obligation of keeping up with the fragile harmony between the apparent and imperceptible powers that shape their reality.

The Achuar nation of Ecuador, living together as one with their unblemished rainforest environmental factors, view the fog as a gatekeeper of biodiversity. Hazy mornings are the point at which the rainforest uncovers its insider facts, exhibiting the many-sided snare of life that relies upon the balance kept up with by native practices. The Achuar perceive that fog assumes a part in supporting the different biological systems they call home, and their conventional land the board rehearses mirror a promise to safeguarding the fragile equilibrium.

Interconnectedness of All Life:

Native points of view on fog highlight a significant comprehension of the interconnectedness of all life. The fog, with its capacity to contact each leaf, each animal, and each soul, turns into an illustration for the complicated dance of connections that characterize the Amazonian environments. The Matsés public, dwelling in the borderlands of Peru and Brazil, express this interconnectedness through their idea of "ayi," which alludes to the daily routine power that moves through all experiencing creatures.

In the fog loaded scenes, the Matsés perceive the strings that wind around together the vegetation, fauna, and human networks. The fog turns into the medium through which the existence force flows, helping them to remember their job as overseers of this perplexing web. Native customs, based on the fog, underscore the correspondence among people and nature, recognizing that each activity swells through the interconnected embroidery of life.

Social Versatility and Opposition:

The foggy domains of the Amazon likewise take the stand concerning the versatility and opposition of native societies. Despite outside pressures, including deforestation, asset extraction, and infringement, fog turns into an image of social grit. The Sápara nation of Ecuador, confronting dangers to their genealogical terrains, draw strength from their profound association with the foggy backwoods.

For the Sápara, fog is a watchman that shroud their customary information, shielding it from outer impacts. It is inside the fog that Sápara older folks pass down the insight of their progenitors to more youthful ages, guaranteeing the congruity of their social practices. The fog, thusly, fills in as a safeguard against social disintegration, exemplifying the opposition of native networks against the powers that try to disturb their lifestyle.

Challenges and the Eventual fate of Cloudy Domains:

Notwithstanding the significant connection between native people groups and fog, the cloudy domains of the Amazon face phenomenal difficulties. Deforestation, driven by logging, horticulture, and framework advancement, takes steps to disentangle the fragile equilibrium that native networks have kept up with for ages. The fog, when an image of congruity, presently looms over scenes scarred by human mediation, seeing the infringement of outer powers.

Environmental change further mixtures the difficulties looked by dim domains. Adjustments in precipitation designs, temperature changes, and the rising recurrence of outrageous climate occasions upset the environmental elements of the rainforest. The fog, personally attached to these biological cycles, turns into a weak component even with worldwide ecological changes.

Native people group, confronting these difficulties, are at the very front of endeavors to safeguard the foggy domains they call home. From pushing for land privileges to taking part in supportable land the board rehearses, native people groups are effectively molding the eventual fate of the fog loaded scenes. The fog, as both observer and member, turns into a mobilizing point for strength and assurance despite outer dangers.

Gatekeepers of the Hazy Domains

In the complex dance between native networks and the hazy domains of the Amazon, a significant story unfurls — one of profound association, social flexibility, and natural stewardship. Fog, to these networks, is certainly not a latent meteorological peculiarity however a living element that reinvigorates the rainforest.

As native points of view on the enchanted characteristics of Amazonian fog uncover, the fog is an entryway, a healer, a courier, and a watchman. A power interfaces ages, domains, and universes. In embracing the fog, native people groups track down strength, shrewdness, and reason — a reason that reaches out past their networks to the more extensive worldwide story of biological protection and social variety.

In the foggy domains of the Amazon, native societies stand as gatekeepers, of their genealogical grounds as well as of the widespread rules that help mankind to remember its interconnectedness with the regular world. As the fog rises and scatters, it abandons a tradition of shrewdness, strength, and a call to safeguard the supernatural characteristics that make the Amazon a safe-haven for both unmistakable and immaterial legacy.

Defending the Hallowed: Native Methodologies for Fog Preservation

In the dim domains of the Amazon, where native networks entwine their lives with the ethereal dance of garoa, the difficulties of ecological preservation are unpredictably woven into their everyday presence. As gatekeepers of the cloudy scenes, native people groups have formulated remarkable procedures to protect the actual environments as well as the otherworldly and social aspects that the fog addresses. These systems, established in customary information and flexibility, stand as a demonstration of the entwined connection between the watchmen of the fog and the actual fog.

Land Guardianship and Local area Based Protection:

Native people group in the Amazon have long perceived the characteristic association among land and culture. The fog loaded scenes are the setting for social practices as well as the stage whereupon native personalities are ordered. Perceiving the inescapable dangers presented by outside powers, especially the infringement of logging and farming, native people groups have accepted the responsibility of land guardianship.

Local area based protection drives, drove by native associations, center around saving huge scopes of rainforest and dim domains. The Kofán nation in Ecuador, for instance, laid out the Sapara Kichwa Territorial Association (SARAKU), an aggregate exertion pointed toward safeguarding their familial grounds from outer double-dealing. Through the boundary of domains and the execution of economical land the board rehearses, these native watchmen guarantee that the fog stays undisturbed, supporting the fragile harmony between the apparent and imperceptible domains.

Lawful Support for Land Privileges:

The dim domains of the Amazon have seen a long history of battles for land privileges by native networks. Perceiving the basic job that fog plays in their social and profound practices, as well as its environmental importance, native pioneers have become strong promoters for lawful acknowledgment of their domains. Land division and insurance are key to their endeavors to safeguard the fog loaded scenes from the infringement of outside powers.

In Brazil, the Munduruku public have been at the very front of fights in court for the boundary of their tribal terrains. The Munduruku, confronting dangers from mining exercises and deforestation, stress the requirement for lawful acknowledgment and security of their fog covered domains. By taking part in lawful backing, native networks state their privileges as stewards of the fog, testing rehearses that risk the fragile equilibrium kept up with by their customary land the executives frameworks.

Maintainable Asset The board:

Native guardianship reaches out past regional division to supportable asset the board rehearses that blend with the cloudy environments.

The idea of "Buen Vivir" or "Sumak Kawsay," embraced by numerous Amazonian native networks, underlines living together as one with nature. It includes rehearses that guarantee the fog isn't just moderated however exists together with flourishing biological systems.

The Sarayaku nation in Ecuador epitomize this methodology through their feasible asset the executives techniques. Perceiving the interconnectedness of the fog with the strength of their properties, the Sarayaku execute customary agroforestry procedures that advance biodiversity and moderate deforestation. By cultivating a complementary relationship with the fog, they save their social legacy as well as add to the general strength of the Amazonian biological systems.

Social Rejuvenation and Instruction:

Native guardianship of the fog isn't exclusively centered around actual protection yet in addition stretches out to social renewal and training. The fog, as a living substance, holds social importance that rises above ages. Native people group comprehend that protecting the fog includes encouraging a comprehension of its profound and social aspects among their childhood.

Drives like the foundation of social focuses, customary schools, and intergenerational information trade programs make light of a critical job in passing the insight related with fog to more youthful ages. The Asháninka public, for example, focus on social schooling for of guaranteeing that the fog keeps on being viewed as meteorological peculiarities as well as a sacrosanct power profoundly weaved with their personality.

Eco-The travel industry as a Device for Protection:

In perceiving the possible financial worth of cloudy scenes, native networks have investigated feasible eco-the travel industry for of creating pay while saving their regions. Eco-the travel industry, when drawn closer carefully and with social responsiveness, turns into a device for both protection and social trade. By welcoming guests to encounter the hazy domains in manners that regard native customs, networks can feature the characteristic worth of their regions.

The Yawanawá nation in Brazil have embraced eco-the travel industry as a procedure to support their networks while bringing issues to light about fog preservation financially. Guests are directed through cloudy woods, participating in functions and social exercises that encourage an appreciation for the interconnectedness of the fog with native societies. The monetary advantages got from eco-the travel industry add to the monetary independence of the local area, reinforcing their capacity to safeguard the fog loaded scenes.

Global Coordinated efforts and Backing:

Perceiving the worldwide meaning of the Amazon rainforest and its dim domains, native networks have participated in global coordinated efforts and promotion endeavors.

These drives mean to accumulate support from the worldwide local area, bring issues to light about the difficulties looked by native people groups, and backer for arrangements that focus on fog preservation and the prosperity of rainforest biological systems.

Native pioneers, like the Kichwa heads of Sarayaku, have effectively taken part in worldwide discussions and meetings to enhance their voices. By manufacturing unions with non-legislative associations, ecological activists, and policymakers, native watchmen look to impact dynamic cycles that influence cloudy scenes. The fog turns into an image of shared liability, rising above lines and calling for aggregate activity despite natural difficulties.

Supporting the Guardianship of the Fog

The foggy domains of the Amazon, supported in the arms of native gatekeepers, give testimony regarding a multi-layered way to deal with protection — one that is well established in social, otherworldly, and natural contemplations. Native people group, as stewards of the fog, explore the fragile dance among custom and variation, versatility and opposition.

As these watchmen carry out methodologies to protect the fog, they offer important examples to the more extensive worldwide local area. The fog turns into an illustration for the interconnectedness of all life, encouraging humankind to perceive its job as overseers of the planet. In supporting the guardianship of the fog, native networks enlighten a way ahead — one that embraces variety, praises custom, and spots the prosperity of the Earth at the very front of our shared perspective.

Chapter 4

African Vistas
Sahara's Silent Sands

African Vistas: Sahara's Quiet Sands

In the core of the African mainland, a huge scope of parched excellence unfurls — the Sahara Desert, a domain of quiet sands and entrancing scenes. This unfriendly yet charming wild stretches across northern Africa, making a permanent imprint on the locale's geology, environment, and societies. As we adventure into the Sahara's quiet sands, a story of topographical marvels, traveling customs, and the fragile dance of life in outrageous circumstances unfurls.

A Geographical Embroidery:

The Sahara, frequently depicted as the world's biggest hot desert, is a geographical embroidery that recounts the tale of old scenes and climatic movements. Crossing around 3.6 million square miles, the Sahara reaches out across Algeria, Chad, Egypt, Libya, Mali, Mauritania, Morocco, Niger, Western Sahara, Sudan, and Tunisia. While regularly connected with vast hills, the Sahara's geography is undeniably more assorted, highlighting rough levels, mountain ranges, and sweeping rock fields.

One of the Sahara's topographical marvels is the Tassili n'Ajjer level in southeastern Algeria. This huge sandstone level, enhanced with dreamlike stone developments and old petroglyphs, offers a brief look into the ancient past of the locale. The dissolved scenes of Tassili n'Ajjer, etched by wind and time, grandstand the Sahara's consistently changing face and the engraving of human home going back millennia.

Migrant Customs:

In the midst of the quiet sands of the Sahara, migrant networks have flourished for quite a long time, epitomizing flexibility and versatility notwithstanding outrageous circumstances. The Tuareg public, frequently alluded to as the "Blue Individuals" because of the indigo color of their customary clothing, are roaming Berber people group tracked down across the Sahara. These talented desert pilots have crossed the huge regions of the Sahara for ages, depending on their profound information on the landscape and divine route.

The Tuareg's roaming way of life is complicatedly connected to the rhythms of the desert. Convoys of camels, weighed down with products, cross antiquated shipping lanes that interface Saharan desert springs and settlements. The Tuareg's authority of endurance in the unforgiving desert climate, from finding water sources to exploring sand hills, represents the significant association between human networks and the Sahara's quiet sands.

Desert springs of Life:

In opposition to the normal impression of a solid ocean of sand, the Sahara harbors stowed away gems — desert gardens that accentuate the parched scene like verdant islands. These pockets of richness, supported by underground springs, have been indispensable helps for both traveling networks and different verdure adjusted to bone-dry circumstances.

One such desert spring is the Siwa Desert spring in Egypt, settled between the Qattara Misery and the Incomparable Sand Ocean. Encircled by tremendous ridges, Siwa is a shelter of date palms, olive forests, and freshwater springs. The old town of Siwa, with its mud-block engineering, remains as a demonstration of the getting through presence of human settlements amidst the Sahara's impressive destruction.

Murmurs of History in the Libyan Desert:

The Libyan Desert, a huge piece of the Sahara spreading over Egypt and Libya, holds reverberations of a former period. Profound inside its quiet sands lie remainders of an old human progress — the Incomparable Sand Ocean, an ocean of rises that hides archeological fortunes underneath its undulating surface. Here, the remainders of failed to remember urban communities and shipping lanes tell stories of a dynamic past.

The lost desert garden of Zerzura, frequently alluded to as the "Desert spring of Birds," is a legendary city supposed to be concealed inside the immensity of the Incomparable Sand Ocean. While its presence remains covered in secret, the charm of Zerzura addresses the Sahara's job as a store of both verifiable stories and tempting secrets.

Transient Excellence of Sand Ridges:

Overwhelmed by a huge ocean of hills, the ergs, the Sahara features the vaporous magnificence of moving sands chiseled by the consistently present breeze. Erg Chebbi in Morocco, with its transcending orange-toned hills, represents the notorious picture of the Sahara. These ridges, some arriving at levels of more than 500 feet, make an entrancing scene that changes with the point of the sun, creating undulating shaded areas and uncovering the complexities of wind-shaped swells.

The rises, frequently viewed as static substances, are in an unending condition of movement. The breezes, known as harmattan in the western piece of the Sahara, consistently reshape the ridges, making a dynamic and steadily changing mosaic of bends and peaks. This ease of structure reflects the transient idea of the Sahara's scenes and the versatility expected for life in this brutal climate.

Outrageous Environment and Climatic Peculiarities:

The Sahara's quiet sands are portrayed by an outrageous environment, with singing temperatures during the day and plunging temperatures around evening time. The immense temperature differentials add to the arrangement of climatic peculiarities that characterize the Sahara's skies.

One such peculiarity is the optical deception known as the "Fata Morgana." This delusion happens when light is refracted through air layers of fluctuating temperatures, making misshaped pictures of far off objects. In the Sahara, where immense spans of level territory meet the sky, the Fata Morgana can change the desert scene into strange and fantastical dreams, obscuring the limits among the real world and deception.

Desert Widely varied vegetation:

As opposed to its apparently desolate appearance, the Sahara upholds an astonishing variety of greenery adjusted to outrageous circumstances. Strong plant species, for example, the dry season safe acacia trees and date palms, dab the scene. These plants have advanced components to monitor water and flourish in the parched climate.

The Sahara is likewise home to one of a kind creature transformations. The fennec fox, with its enormous ears for heat dissemination, and the addax impala, equipped for making due without water for broadened periods, are instances of the exceptional variations that empower life to persevere in this difficult climate.

Also, transitory birds, for example, the more noteworthy hoopoe-songbird, navigate the Sahara, using desert gardens as fundamental lay stops on their excursions.

Stargazing and Heavenly Association:

The Sahara's quiet sands have filled in as a heavenly material for centuries, offering unhindered perspectives on the night sky. Roaming societies, like the Tuareg, have created mind boggling information on divine route, involving stars as guides across the featureless regions of the desert.

The Ténéré Desert in Niger, some portion of the bigger Sahara, is eminent for its dull skies and is viewed as perhaps of the best put on Earth for stargazing. The Ténéré's immeasurability and low light contamination make an unrivaled divine scene, where heavenly bodies, planets, and the Smooth Way are apparent with momentous clearness. The heavenly association of the Sahara mirrors the significant connection between desert-abiding networks and the inestimable rhythms that oversee their lifestyle.

Social Legacy and Oral Customs:

The Sahara's quiet sands reverberation with the voices of different societies and the oral customs went down through ages. Migrant people group, like the Berbers and Tuareg, have safeguarded their narratives, fantasies, and strategy for practical adaptations through oral narrating. These accounts, frequently joined by music and verse, add to the rich social embroidery of the Sahara.

The Tifinagh script, utilized by the Tuareg, is an extraordinary putting down framework that has been utilized to account and send information across the ages. The stone craftsmanship tracked down in different pieces of the Sahara, including Tassili n'Ajjer, fills in as a visual demonstration of the old developments that once thrived in this imposing scene.

Natural Difficulties and Preservation Endeavors:

While the Sahara's quiet sands inspire a feeling of immortal magnificence, they likewise give testimony regarding contemporary natural difficulties. Desertification, exacerbated by elements, for example, environmental change and unreasonable land use rehearses, represents a danger to the delicate biological systems of the Sahara. The extension of human exercises, including agribusiness and framework advancement, further strains the sensitive equilibrium of this bone-dry area.

Endeavors to address these difficulties incorporate drives zeroed in on maintainable land the board, reforestation, and local area based preservation. Associations and nearby networks are cooperating to execute techniques that advance flexibility and safeguard the novel biodiversity of the Sahara. These undertakings perceive the interconnectedness of the Sahara's biological systems with worldwide ecological elements.

Ways of the world and Getting through Soul

As we cross the Sahara's quiet sands, we experience a land wonder as well as a living demonstration of the perseverance of life in outrageous circumstances. The quiet sands, molded by the powers of wind and time, harbor a variety of biological systems and societies that have adjusted to the difficulties of the desert. From roaming customs to divine associations, the Sahara's scenes offer bits of knowledge into the unpredictable dance among nature and humankind.

The sands of the Sahara, steadily moving and ageless, give testimony regarding the section of centuries. However, in the midst of the hills and rough levels, life continues in structures both versatile and versatile. The persevering through soul of roaming networks, the secret fortunes underneath the sand, and the heavenly stories written in the night sky all add to the Sahara's persona.

In pondering the Sahara's quiet sands, we wind up brought into a story that rises above the limits of topography and time. It is an account of endurance, social extravagance, and the significant interconnectedness among mankind and the regular world. The Sahara allures us to pay attention to its murmurs conveyed by the breeze, to stroll in the strides of travelers, and to look at the heavenly miracles that have directed endless excursions across the quiet spread of the desert.

4.1 Unraveling the enigmatic mists of the Sahara Desert.

Unwinding the Perplexing Fogs of the Sahara Desert

In the aggregate creative mind, the Sahara Desert frequently summons pictures of vast rises and sun-burned scenes. In any case, inside this immense span of parched magnificence lies a peculiarity that overcomes traditional presumption — the baffling fogs of the Sahara. A long way from the cliché vision of an unwelcoming and forlorn desert, the Sahara uncovers a nuanced and perplexing side, where brief fogs wind through the quiet sands, making a permanent imprint on the district's environment, biological systems, and social stories.

The Delusion of Fogs:

The presence of fogs in the Sahara, however irregular and vaporous, adds an ethereal quality to its scenes. One of the most enamoring indications of these fogs is the optical peculiarity known as the hallucination. In the Sahara's searing intensity, the connection between the sun and the desert floor makes delusions that pull pranks on the spectator's discernment.

As the sun's beams heat the outer layer of the desert, the air above turns out to be unevenly warmed, making light refract in manners that make deceptions of water or far off desert springs.

Explorers in the Sahara have described delusions that apparently change the parched field into lakes or lavish vegetation, just to scatter after looking into it further. This delusion of fogs, brought into the world from the complicated dance of light and intensity, adds to the Sahara's persona, obscuring the limits among the real world and deception.

The Dance of Harmattan Winds:

While the Sahara is prestigious for its extraordinary intensity, likewise impacted by environmental peculiarities present a component of dampness and, thusly, fog. The harmattan twists, starting from the Sahara and blowing towards the Atlantic Sea, assume a vital part in forming the desert's environment. These dry and dusty exchange twists, loaded down with fine particles from the desert floor, navigate immense distances, affecting both the Sahara and the districts they experience.

Throughout the cold weather months, the harmattan twists clear across the Sahara, conveying dust particles that can darken perceivability and make a murky air. Notwithstanding, as these breezes travel over cooler waterways, for example, the Bay of Guinea, they go through a change. The cooperation with the sea's dampness permits the harmattan to get stickiness, prompting the development of fog. This fog loaded harmattan, while still a generally dry peculiarity, carries an unpretentious bit of dampness to the bone-dry scenes it crosses.

Desert springs in the Fog:

In the midst of the quiet sands of the Sahara, desert springs stand as verdant safe-havens, frequently hidden in hazy appeal. These asylums of life, supported by underground springs, intersperse the desert's tremendousness with pockets of fruitfulness. The presence of fog in these desert gardens isn't just a climatic idiosyncrasy yet a crucial component in supporting the different biological systems that flourish in these segregated scenes.

Siwa Desert spring in Egypt, settled between the Qattara Sadness and the Incomparable Sand Ocean, epitomizes the desert spring persona in the Sahara. Encircled by transcending ridges, Siwa becomes wrapped in fog during specific seasons, making a captivating vibe. The fog not just adds a dreamlike wonder to the desert garden yet additionally assumes a pivotal part in supporting the lavish vegetation and date palm forests that characterize Siwa's personality. It is a sensitive exchange of environment, geology, and human connection that changes desert gardens into fog covered shelters in the core of the desert.

Itinerant Points of view on Sahara's Fogs:

For the itinerant networks that have navigated the Sahara for quite a long time, the presence of fog holds social importance past its meteorological perspectives. The Tuareg, frequently alluded to as the "Blue Individuals" because of the indigo color of their conventional clothing, are migrant Berber people group with a profound association with the desert's rhythms, including its incidental fogs.

In Tuareg fables, the desert fogs are accepted to be shroud that hide concealed domains and ethereal aspects. The moving sands, when hidden in fog, are considered a liminal space where the limits between the substantial and the otherworldly haze. Traveling customs, services, and narrating frequently track down reverberation with the puzzling fogs, as they become an illustration for the transient idea of life in the Sahara and the interconnectedness of the itinerant networks with their steadily evolving climate.

Fogs in the Sahara's Social Woven artwork:

The Sahara's fogs are woven into the social embroidery of the networks that have called this tremendous desert home for ages. In the oral practices of the Saharan people groups, fogs are not only meteorological occasions but rather substances with emblematic and otherworldly aspects. The Tifinagh script, utilized by the Tuareg, is a demonstration of the Sahara's getting through social legacy, catching the subtleties of life in the desert, including its fog loaded minutes.

Rock workmanship tracked down in different pieces of the Sahara, like Tassili n'Ajjer in Algeria, portrays scenes of human existence, untamed life, and the desert's steadily evolving conditions. These old portrayals, carved into the stones by the Sahara's earliest occupants, offer looks into the social importance appended to regular peculiarities, including the fogs that incidentally elegance the desert's scenes.

Fleeting Magnificence of Cloudy Ridges:

The Sahara's notorious ridges, etched by the breeze, take on another aspect when hidden in fog. While the exemplary picture of transcending sand hills against a background of clear blue skies is without a doubt charming, the exchange of fog with the ridges adds a transient delight to this parched scene. Erg Chebbi in Morocco, with its orange-shaded hills, turns into a dreamlike and extraordinary domain when fog dives upon its quiet sands.

The smoothness of structure that portrays sand hills is complemented when fog winds through their peaks and valleys. The play of light and shadow, diffused through the fog, changes the ridges into a steadily moving material of surfaces and tones. The Sahara's fog loaded ridges, a long way from static substances, become dynamic scenes that spellbind the faculties and move consideration.

Climatic Elements and Fog Development:

The development of fogs in the Sahara is unpredictably connected to the desert's climatic elements, which are impacted by a blend of geological highlights and worldwide air designs. The Tibesti Mountains, Hoggar Mountains, and Ahaggar Mountains, among others, add to the Sahara's changed geography, affecting temperature differentials and wind designs.

The connection of these geographic elements with the overall exchange twists, like the harmattan, makes microclimates inside the Sahara. At the point when these breezes experience cooler waterways, dampness is brought high up, prompting the development of fog. While the Sahara is described by its dry environment, an intermittent union of these air components leads to the magical presence of fogs that effortlessness its scenes.

Fogs as Environment Pointers:

Past their stylish and social importance, the fogs of the Sahara likewise act as marks of more extensive climatic changes. The Sahara is no more odd to the effects of environmental change, with studies proposing shifts in precipitation designs, expanded temperatures, and the infringement of desertification. Noticing the recurrence and conveyance of fogs in the Sahara furnishes scientists with significant bits of knowledge into the perplexing transaction between barometrical circumstances and the desert's natural equilibrium.

Logical undertakings, including satellite perceptions and environment displaying, add to how we might interpret how the Sahara answers ecological movements. A periodic cloudy episodes become necessary pieces in the riddle of unwinding the perplexing connections between the Sahara's environment, air elements, and the more extensive setting of worldwide environmental change.

Protection Contemplations:

As the Sahara's fogs wind through its scenes, they highlight the sensitive equilibrium that characterizes the desert's biological systems. Protection endeavors in the Sahara should not just location the apparent difficulties, like desertification and environment debasement, yet in addition consider the nuanced transaction of climatic elements that impact the district's biodiversity.

Supportable land the board rehearses, reforestation drives, and local area based protection endeavors become fundamental parts of defending the Sahara's remarkable biological systems. Perceiving the social meaning of fogs to the desert's native networks, protection systems ought to likewise incorporate customary environmental information and traveling viewpoints to guarantee an all encompassing and comprehensive way to deal with saving the Sahara's quiet sands and their perplexing fogs.

Hidden Murmurs in the Desert Wind

In unwinding the puzzling fogs of the Sahara Desert, we find a domain where the noticeable and imperceptible entwine, where temporary snapshots of barometrical beauty leave a persevering through influence on the scenes and societies that call this parched spread home. The fogs become hidden murmurs in the desert wind, conveying with them the accounts of migrants, the social extravagance of Saharan people group, and the quiet excellence of fog loaded rises.

As we consider the Sahara's fogs, we are welcome to rise above assumptions of devastation and fruitlessness. All things considered, we experience a desert that is dynamic, versatile, and personally associated with the climatic complexities of our planet. An intermittent fog that graces the Sahara's quiet sands turns into an illustration for the transient idea of magnificence, the flexibility of life, and the persevering through soul of a scene that proceeds to enamor and beguile the people who adventure into its endlessness.

Social Resonations: Past Meteorology

The social resonations of the Sahara's fogs stretch out a long ways past their meteorological ramifications. In the stories of the Sahara's native networks, fog turns into a figurative extension between the substantial and the immaterial, the seen and the concealed. For the Tuareg, the fog loaded ridges are not simply actual scenes; they are limits to the profound domain, where the cloak between the material and the ethereal is flimsy.

The Tuareg's migrant way of life, unpredictably weaved with the Sahara's rhythms, tracks down articulation in their creative customs. Tifinagh, the old content utilized by the Tuareg, turns into a vehicle for recording the unmistakable parts of desert life as well as the fleeting experiences with fogs and hallucinations. Rock etchings in Tassili n'Ajjer catch the dance of fog through the ages, offering looks into how these networks see and connect with the tricky peculiarity.

Social celebrations and services, for example, the Tuareg's Takoubelt and the Kel Essuf, frequently integrate representative components connected with fogs. The cadenced pounding of drums, the ululations that penetrate the quietness of the desert air, and the twirling dance of hidden calculates all become demonstrations of social praise to the baffling fogs that effortlessness the Sahara. At these times, fog rises above its meteorological nature to turn into a living substance — a member in the social embroidery of the Sahara.

Roaming Intelligence: Exploring Life's Fogs

The migrant networks of the Sahara, especially the Tuareg, have improved an extraordinary arrangement of abilities to explore the actual devastation of the desert as well as life's figurative fogs. The capacity to peruse the signs in the sand, decipher the moving breezes, and perceive the unpretentious signals of nature turns into a type of traveling shrewdness went down through ages.

In the Sahara's steadily evolving scenes, where the line among endurance and affliction is flimsy, the travelers track down strength in their flexibility. Fog, as far as they might be concerned, isn't a deterrent however an aide — a sign that the sensitive harmony between dampness and aridity is influencing everything. The migrant insight encapsulated by these networks shows us about actual endurance in outrageous conditions as well as about versatility, creativity, and the ability to track down magnificence in the short lived nature of life.

Natural Dance: Fog as a Life saver for Biodiversity

The fogs that elegance the Sahara are an exhibition for the natural eye as well as a life saver for the desert's exceptional biodiversity. A periodic dampness presented by fogs turns into a valuable asset for vegetation adjusted to parched conditions. Plant species, for example, the tough acacia trees, draw food from the dampness, guaranteeing the endurance of environments that seem barren right away.

The Sahara's natural life, including the fennec fox and addax pronghorn, has developed to flourish in conditions where water is scant. These animals show exceptional transformations that permit them to get through the difficulties of the desert, and the irregular fogs give vital snapshots of alleviation. Transitory birds, exploring the huge territory of the Sahara, use desert springs framed by fog as vital visits in their excursions.

In the biological dance of the Sahara, fog arises as a central participant — a vaporous supporter that supports life against the background of brutal circumstances. Protection endeavors, subsequently, should address the noticeable dangers to biodiversity as well as recognize the unobtrusive natural subtleties related with fog development and its effect on the sensitive equilibrium of desert environments.

Climatic Riddles: Sahara's Fogs in an Impacting World

As our planet goes through significant climatic movements, the Sahara's fogs become pieces in a bigger riddle — a riddle that researchers and specialists are determinedly attempting to unravel. A periodic hazy episodes in the Sahara offer significant experiences into the mind boggling elements of environmental change and its repercussions on provincial and worldwide scales.

The Sahara, generally saw as an image of aridity and intensity, is encountering changes in precipitation examples and temperature systems. These changes, entwined with more extensive environment shifts, impact the recurrence and force of fogs in the desert. Concentrating on the fogs of the Sahara turns into a focal point through which researchers can notice the effects of environmental change on bone-dry conditions and gain a more profound comprehension of the unpredictable connections between barometrical circumstances and earthly scenes.

Additionally, the Sahara's fogs add to conversations on worldwide environment designs and barometrical course. The harmattan winds, which assume a part in fog development, are important for a bigger air framework that interfaces landmasses. As environment researchers dig into the intricacies of these frameworks, the Sahara's fogs become marks of climatic complexities that stretch out past territorial lines.

The Fate of Sahara's Fogs: Supporting Mindfulness and Preservation

The eventual fate of the Sahara's fogs is weaved with more extensive discussions about ecological mindfulness, protection, and feasible practices. In a world wrestling with the difficulties of environmental change, desertification, and biodiversity misfortune, the fogs of the Sahara become symbolic of the interconnectedness between human activities and the prosperity of our planet.

Sustaining mindfulness about the social, environmental, and climatic meaning of the Sahara's fogs turns into a critical stage in cultivating a feeling of obligation and stewardship. Drives that join logical examination, native information, and local area commitment can add to a comprehensive way to deal with fog preservation.

Protection endeavors shouldn't just zero in on moderating the apparent effects of environmental change yet additionally embrace the nuances related with fog arrangement and its job in keeping up with the sensitive equilibrium of desert biological systems. Supporting roaming networks and native points of view, which have supported the Sahara's fogs for a really long time, becomes fundamental to any preservation system.

The baffling fogs of the Sahara Desert allure us to investigate the convergences of culture, nature, and environment. They advise us that even in the apparently cold boundlessness of a desert, there exists a sensitive dance of life — a dance wherein fogs assume an essential and frequently disregarded part. As we disentangle the secrets of the Sahara's fogs, we uncover the insider facts of the desert as well as the multifaceted strings that interface mankind to the more extensive embroidered artwork of our planet.

4.2 Examining how mist transforms the vast dunes and ancient landscapes.

Analyzing the Groundbreaking Dance of Fog: Sahara's Tremendous Rises and Antiquated Scenes

The Sahara Desert, with its sweeping ocean of rises and old scenes, presents a material where nature, time, and environmental components meet in a hypnotizing exhibition. Vital to this mysterious venue is the groundbreaking dance of fog, a transient peculiarity that winds through the quiet sands, making a permanent imprint on the Sahara's immense rises and the persevering through stories carved into its old scenes.

The Quiet Stage: Sahara's Sweeping Hills

To grasp the extraordinary force of fog in the Sahara, one must initially imagine the quiet stage whereupon this climatic artful dance unfurls — the immense ridges that characterize the desert's notorious symbolism.

Ergs, or sand oceans, for example, Erg Chebbi in Morocco and the Incomparable Sand Ocean in Egypt, present undulating scenes where transcending ridges rise like titanic waves frozen in time. These ridges, etched by the persistent touch of the breeze, are not static substances but rather unique developments in a ceaseless condition of motion.

The Sahara's hills are described by their sheer scale, some arriving at levels of more than 500 feet, and their multifaceted examples formed by the interchange of wind and sand. Erg Chebbi, with its brilliant toned hills, embodies the quintessential Sahara postcard picture. As the sun navigates the sky, creating steadily changing shaded areas and featuring the bends and peaks of the rises, the stage is set for the extraordinary entry of fog — a peculiarity that modifies discernments and upgrades the beautiful magnificence of the desert.

The Vaporous Expressive dance: Fog and Ridges as one

Fog, frequently connected with clammy and mild environments, may appear to be incongruent with the bone-dry climate of the Sahara. In any case, it is exactly this startling experience that leads to a stunning dance of differentiations. The fog, when it graces the Sahara's ridges, obscures the lines among earth and sky, changing the natural into the dreamlike.

In Erg Chebbi, for example, the entry of fog changes the ridges into ethereal models. The dampness loaded air relax the sharp edges of the sand, making an extraordinary atmosphere. What was once a scene of obvious differences turns into a dreamscape where the limits between the substantial and the immaterial are obscured. The ridges, covered in fog, appear to stretch out into vastness, welcoming examination and thought-fulness.

The fog confers a diffused quality to the daylight, giving occasion to feel qualms about a delicate sparkle the ridges. The exchange of light and fog makes a chiaroscuro impact, highlighting the forms of the ridges while veiling far off skylines in a sensitive murkiness. Erg Chebbi, hung in fog, turns into a domain where time seems to stop — a demonstration of the fleeting idea of excellence and the extraordinary impact of climatic components on the desert's excellent stage.

Worldly Speculative chemistry: Fog and the Hallucination Delusion, the Deception of Desert garden

One of the most charming impacts of fog in the Sahara is the production of delusions — a peculiarity where far off objects, frequently waterways or rich vegetation, show up as ethereal deceptions. This transient speculative chemistry, brought into the world from the interchange of light, heat, and climatic circumstances, adds to the persona of the Sahara's old scenes.

As fog cover the far off scopes of the desert, hallucinations appear not too far off, enticing explorers with deceptions of desert spring like heavens. The delusion, a result of refracted light in the warm desert air, has been a wellspring of interest and old stories all through mankind's set of experiences.

In the Sahara, where water is a valuable ware and desert gardens are helps in the immense region, fog prompted hallucinations become both an idyllic reflecting of human longings and a demonstration of the Sahara's capacity to dumbfound and perplex.

Travelers navigating the quiet sands, directed by the stars and the forms of the rises, have experienced delusions that obscure the limits among the real world and deception. The charm of a desert spring sparkling somewhere far off, just to evaporate upon approach, turns into a representation for the transient idea of life in the Sahara — a consistent journey for food and safe-haven in a scene that the two gives and holds back.

Transient Speculative chemistry: Fog and the Hallucination Delusion, the Deception of Desert garden

One of the most captivating impacts of fog in the Sahara is the production of delusions — a peculiarity where far off objects, frequently waterways or rich vegetation, show up as ethereal deceptions. This fleeting speculative chemistry, brought into the world from the interaction of light, heat, and barometrical circumstances, adds to the persona of the Sahara's antiquated scenes.

As fog cover the far off ranges of the desert, delusions emerge not too far off, tempting explorers with deceptions of desert garden like heavens. The delusion, a result of refracted light in the warm desert air, has been a wellspring of interest and legends all through mankind's set of experiences. In the Sahara, where water is a valuable product and desert gardens are helps in the immense territory, fog prompted illusions become both a beautiful reflecting of human longings and a demonstration of the Sahara's capacity to bewilder and perplex.

Travelers crossing the quiet sands, directed by the stars and the forms of the ridges, have experienced hallucinations that obscure the limits among the real world and deception. The charm of a desert spring shining somewhere far off, just to evaporate upon approach, turns into an illustration for the transient idea of life in the Sahara — a steady mission for food and safe-haven in a scene that the two gives and holds back.

Engineers of Time: Wind, Sand, and Fog as Stone workers

The Sahara's hills, molded by the steady powers of wind and sand, stand as structural wonders etched by the components. In any case, the groundbreaking hint of fog adds a vaporous layer to this amazing plan. Fog, in its fragile hug with the rises, turns into a vaporous craftsman, complementing the shapes and uncovering the many-sided subtleties of the desert's ageless figures.

As the fog winds through the ridges, it abandons unobtrusive follows — a delicate kiss that dampens the sand, upgrading its tone and surface. The typically unforgiving and sun-prepared surface of the rises takes on a gentler tint, reflecting the fragile exchange among dampness and aridity.

This powerful connection among fog and sand divulges a range of tones, from warm gold to cool silver, making a visual ensemble that rises above the monochromatic generalization frequently connected with deserts.

In the Hoggar Heaps of Algeria, where old scenes demonstrate the veracity of centuries of geographical changes, fog uncovers the land embroidery with newly discovered clearness. Rock developments, endured by time and the components, rise out of the fog as quiet sentinels, watchmen of the Sahara's profound history. The fog, in this specific circumstance, turns into a fleeting revealer — a medium through which the Sahara's old stories are carved into the actual texture of the desert.

Roaming Strides: Navigating Fog Loaded Hills

For roaming networks that have navigated the Sahara for a really long time, fog isn't only a meteorological event yet a basic piece of their itinerant processes. The Tuareg, Bedouins, and other desert-abiding clans explore the immense hills with a cozy comprehension of the barometrical subtleties, including an intermittent hug of fog.

Travelers, frequently directed by divine route and a significant information on the desert's geography, wind through fog loaded rises with a sharp consciousness of the scene's extraordinary characteristics. Fog, as far as they might be concerned, is both a sidekick and a test — a hidden questioner that acquaints a component of unusualness with their excursions. The migrant strides that mark the sands of the Sahara give testimony regarding an immortal hit the dance floor with fog, a dance that rises above individual lifetimes and interfaces travelers to the getting through soul of the desert.

An Ensemble of Faculties: Fog's Effect on Discernment

In the Sahara, where tactile encounters are elevated by the immeasurability and isolation of the scene, fog turns into a director coordinating an orchestra of faculties. The effect of fog on insight reaches out past the visual, drawing in with the material, hear-able, and olfactory components of the desert.

The hint of fog on the skin, an unpretentious touch that overcomes the parched presumption of the Sahara, makes a tactile oddity. Wanderers, hung in indigo robes and turbaned against the sun, feel the soggy breath of fog amidst a climate familiar with dry breezes and searing intensity. This material irregularity adds a layer of intricacy to the roaming experience, an update that the Sahara's mind-sets are basically as shifted as the grains of sand underneath their feet.

As fog slides upon the ridges, it changes the soundscape of the Sahara. The normally quieted murmurs of the desert are decorated with the delicate mumble of dampness loaded air, making an environmental quiet that intensifies the isolation of the ridges. The wanderers, sensitive to the nuances of the desert's sounds, track down a melodic reverberation in the fog — a characteristic sythesis that orchestrates with the old rhythms of their roaming way of life.

Besides, the scent of fog, an uncommon olfactory guilty pleasure in the bone-dry field, adds a tactile layer to the Sahara's vibe. The fragrance of sodden sand, blending with the hearty smells of desert greenery, makes an olfactory ensemble that waits in the air. Migrants, acclimated with the dry scent of the desert, experience a transient bouquet that goes with them through fog loaded ridges, enhancing their tactile association with the Sahara.

Social Reverberation: Fog in Saharan Folklore and Legends

In the rich embroidery of Saharan folklore and old stories, fog arises as an image weighed down with social reverberation. The accounts of itinerant networks, communicated through ages by means of oral customs, melodies, and ceremonies, frequently mesh fog into the cosmological texture of the Sahara.

For the Tuareg, fog isn't only a meteorological occasion however a shroud that isolates the seen and the inconspicuous. In Tuareg folklore, the desert fogs are entries to ethereal domains, where spirits and divinities live. The moving sands, when hidden in fog, become a liminal space where the limits between the natural and the heavenly haze. The migrants, caretakers of these old fantasies, find otherworldly importance in fog loaded hills — an association with a powerful aspect that rises above the noticeable scenes of the Sahara.

Saharan legends swarms with accounts of migrants experiencing extraordinary creatures, djinn, and genealogical spirits amidst fog loaded hills. These stories, went down through the ages, highlight the close connection between traveling networks and the baffling fogs that elegance their desert home. Fog, in this social setting, is a narrator — a medium through which the travelers draw in with the secrets of their reality and associate with the profound legacy of the Sahara.

The Hallucination of Supportability: Fog as an Impetus forever

While fog in the Sahara might appear to be short lived and ethereal, its effect on the desert's biological systems is significant. A periodic dampness presented by fog turns into an impetus forever, supporting widely varied vegetation that have developed to flourish in dry circumstances. The delusion, a deception brought into the world from fog, changes into a representation for the manageability of life in the desert — a sensitive dance among shortage and overflow.

Desert gardens, those verdant gems settled inside the parched immeasurability of the Sahara, owe their reality to some extent to the extraordinary bit of fog. The dampness loaded air, conveyed by the harmattan winds or created by nearby climatic circumstances, gives a help to these confined biological systems. As migrants approach fog covered hills, they might find stowed away desert gardens that overcome the presumption of a fruitless scene. The illusion turns into a substantial reality — a demonstration of the Sahara's capacity to support life in unforeseen corners of its quiet territory.

The Sahara's untamed life, adjusted to the desert's difficulties, benefits from the irregular dampness presented by fog. Plant species, for example, the strong acacia trees, draw food from the fog, making microenvironments that help different environments. In this sensitive equilibrium, fog turns into an overseer of biodiversity — a fundamental figure the endurance of species that have developed to explore the difficulties of the Sahara's cruel environment.

Protection Contemplations: Supporting the Fog Loaded Sahara

As the Sahara's hills and old scenes keep on enamoring the human creative mind, it becomes basic to consider the preservation of fog loaded conditions. The fragile harmony among dampness and aridity, so fundamental to the supportability of life in the desert, is vulnerable to the effects of environmental change, natural surroundings corruption, and human exercises.

Preservation endeavors should go past conventional standards and envelop the nuanced elements related with fog development in the Sahara. Economical land the executives rehearses, local area based protection drives, and the coordination of native information become fundamental parts of saving fog loaded environments. Perceiving the social meaning of fog in the Sahara, protection procedures ought to likewise include roaming networks as stewards of the desert's antiquated scenes.

Furthermore, the Sahara's part in worldwide environment elements requires a more extensive viewpoint on protection. A periodic dim episodes, entwined with environmental cycles, add to the mind boggling dance of environment designs that rise above territorial boundaries. Protection procedures for the Sahara's fog loaded conditions ought to be educated by a comprehensive comprehension regarding the desert's environmental interconnectedness with the more extensive planet.

Enchanted by a scene that blows some minds and welcomes reflection. The Sahara's fogs, once thought to be transient and irrelevant, arise as overseers of a fragile harmony — the quiet choreographers of an immortal expressive dance between earth, sky, and air.

Exploring the Hidden Unexplored world:

For travelers who navigate the Sahara, the fog loaded ridges address actual milestones as well as gateways to the unexplored world. The cloak of fog, floating through the hills, acquaints a component of vulnerability with their excursions. Traveling insight, sharpened through ages of crossing the quiet sands, helps them to explore the noticeable scenes as well as the hidden secrets disguised by fog.

In the tremendous territory of the Sahara, where the skyline frequently mixes flawlessly with the sky, fog turns into a divine pilot. Travelers, directed by the stars and the forms of fog loaded ridges, depend on their personal information on the desert's steadily evolving subtleties.

Fog, in this specific situation, turns into a heavenly guide — an ethereal aide that upgrades the traveling experience and encourages a profound association between the Sahara's occupants and their desert home.

Worldly Reverberation: Fog and Geographical Time

The Sahara's old scenes, set apart by rock arrangements endured by centuries of land processes, reverberate with fog in manners that rise above the transient idea of barometrical peculiarities. Fog, with its fragile touch, uncovers the land embroidery of the Sahara with a clearness that escapes the brutal light of the sun.

In the Hoggar Heaps of Algeria, where rock craftsmanship gives testimony regarding the Sahara's profound history, fog turns into a fleeting revealer. The old etchings, made by hands a distant memory, rise up out of the fog as quiet observers to the progression of time. The stone developments, etched by the patient stroke of wind and sand, bear the engravings of incalculable years — a demonstration of the persevering through nature of the Sahara's old scenes.

As fog winds through the land arrangements, it appears to mellow the edges of time. The Hoggar Mountains, when seen as emotionless sentinels of the past, take on an ethereal quality that obscures the limits between ages. Fog turns into an assistant to time travel, welcoming consideration on the monstrosity of land processes that have molded the Sahara's ageless sands.

Transient Magnificence: Fog and the Fleeting Idea of Sahara's Imaginativeness

While the Sahara's hills and old scenes stand as getting through landmarks to the powers of nature, fog presents a transient stunner that underlines the fleetingness of even the most great developments. The transaction of fog with the Sahara's fabulous embroidery is an update that magnificence, as well, is dependent upon the impulses of climatic circumstances and the progression of time.

In Erg Chebbi, where the brilliant tinted hills ascend with a practically strange evenness, fog bestows an illusory quality to the scene. The consistently moving shapes of the hills, upgraded by the diffused light of fog, make a creativity that exists in a condition of ceaseless becoming. Erg Chebbi, hung in fog, turns into a residing material where the Sahara's excellence isn't static yet powerful — a demonstration of the transient idea, everything being equal.

Fog, as it wraps the ridges, appears to take part in an exchange with the actual pith of the desert. The Sahara, frequently saw as a domain of constant aridity, uncovers its ability for change when moved by fog. The fleetingness of fog loaded excellence turns into an illustration for the Sahara's capacity to adjust, develop, and embrace the ephemerality innate in the regular world.

Social Coherence: Fog as a String in the Texture of Saharan Life

In the multifaceted texture of Saharan societies, fog arises as a string that ties ages, fantasies, and customs. The migrants, inheritors of a heritage woven into the very sands they track, find coherence and association through the consistently present fog that graces their desert home.

Social ceremonies, for example, the Tuareg's Takoubelt and the Kel Essuf, frequently integrate emblematic components connected with fog. The musical thumps of drums, the ululations that penetrate the quietness of the desert air, and the twirling dance of hidden figures become demonstrations of social tribute to the cryptic fogs that beauty the Sahara. Fog, at these times, isn't just a meteorological event however a member in the social embroidery of the Sahara.

The narrating customs of Saharan travelers, went down through oral stories and creative articulations, are instilled with the persona of fog loaded scenes. Stories of experiences with otherworldly creatures amidst fog loaded rises, or the imagery of fog as a liminal space between the unmistakable and the profound, reverberate across ages. Fog turns into a social course — a component that shapes the stories, values, and personality of Saharan people group.

Preservation Difficulties and Potential open doors: Protecting Fog Loaded Scenes

As fog keeps on winding through the Sahara's huge hills and antiquated scenes, protection endeavors should go up against both the difficulties and potential open doors related with safeguarding these fog loaded conditions. The sensitive harmony among dampness and aridity, basic to the supportability of life in the desert, is vulnerable to the effects of environmental change, natural surroundings debasement, and human exercises.

Preservation systems shouldn't just zero in on the noticeable dangers yet additionally envelop the nuanced elements related with fog arrangement in the Sahara. Economical land the executives rehearses, local area based protection drives, and the mix of native information become fundamental parts of safeguarding fog loaded environments. The social meaning of fog in the Sahara calls for comprehensive protection moves toward that include roaming networks as dynamic members in the stewardship of their old scenes.

Moreover, perceiving the Sahara's job in worldwide environment elements, preservation endeavors ought to take on a comprehensive viewpoint. The Sahara's fogs, interlaced with air processes, add to the multifaceted dance of environment designs that rise above provincial lines. Preservation procedures for fog loaded conditions ought to be educated by a more extensive comprehension regarding the Sahara's environmental interconnectedness with the more extensive planet.

The assessment of how fog changes the immense hills and old scenes of the Sahara uncovers an intricate transaction between the fleeting and the persevering.

Fog, as it graces the Sahara's fantastic stage, turns into a fleeting craftsman, uncovering stowed away features of land time, upgrading the transient magnificence of the desert's creativity, and winding around a social congruity that traverses ages. As the Sahara's fogs keep on spreading out across the ageless sands, they coax us to investigate the noticeable scenes as well as the elusive domains of social legacy, land stories, and the sensitive dance among supportability and ephemerality in the core of the desert.

4.3 Stories of nomadic cultures and their relationship with desert mists.

Roaming Stories: An Embroidery of Stories Woven in Fog

In the tremendous and immortal scenes of deserts, roaming societies have scratched their accounts into the actual texture of the dry earth. These accounts, went down through ages, are stories of versatility, transformation, and a personal hit the dance floor with the hard to find fog that graces the desert domains. The narratives of migrant societies and their relationship with desert fogs unfurl as an embroidery, each string uncovering a novel feature of the mind boggling and persevering through association among people and the supernatural cloak that float through the rises.

Saharan Wanderers: Gatekeepers of the Quiet Sands

In the Sahara, where the quiet of the sands is just broken by the murmuring breezes and the delicate footfalls of wanderers, the relationship with desert fogs is significant. The Tuareg, frequently called the "Blue Individuals" for their indigo-colored pieces of clothing, are among the Sahara's watchmen, winding around a traveling presence that has persevered for a really long time. For these travelers, the fog isn't simply a meteorological event; it is a quiet sidekick in their perpetual excursion across the quiet sands.

The stories of the Tuareg, went down through oral practices, talk about fog loaded ridges as holy spaces where the shroud between the natural and the otherworldly is slim. In the hug of fog, wanderers wind up in a liminal domain, where the seen and the concealed join. The fog turns into an aide, a covered partner that coordinates their migrant strides across the tremendous material of the Sahara.

Exploring by the Stars and Fog: The Craft of Roaming Wayfinding

Itinerant societies, innately attached to the extensive deserts, have created complicated abilities to explore the apparently featureless scenes. Directed by the divine dance of stars and the nuances of the desert geography, migrants navigate the hills with a significant comprehension of the barometrical subtleties, including a periodic presence of fog.

In the Sahara, where tourist spots are scant and the skyline appears to be unfathomable, migrants have excelled at wayfinding through the fog loaded ridges.

The dampness loaded air modifies the tangible scene, offering unobtrusive prompts that migrants decipher with an expertise sharpened over ages. The hint of fog on the skin, the fragrance of hosed sand, and the quieted soundscape add to a roaming ensemble that guides them through the hidden fields of the desert.

Hallucinations and Secrets: Traveling Experiences in Fog Loaded Domains

Roaming ventures through fog loaded deserts frequently include experiences with delusions — deceptions that dance not too far off, prodding the faculties with commitments of desert spring like heavens. These hallucinations, brought into the world from the exchange of fog, daylight, and intensity, have become vital to the migrant experience, implanting themselves in the legend and legends of desert societies.

Wanderers, navigating the quiet sands, have woven stories of delusions that entice from a good ways, just to disseminate upon approach. These accounts become representations for the transient idea of life in the desert — a consistent journey for food and safe-haven in a scene that the two gives and holds back. The hallucination, rising up out of the fog, turns into a friend in the migrant excursion — an image of the hidden secrets that the desert holds.

Tuareg Ceremonies: Fog as an Otherworldly Cover

For the Tuareg wanderers, fog isn't only a meteorological event; a profound peculiarity rises above the actual domain. Tuareg customs, profoundly interlaced with the migrant lifestyle, frequently consolidate emblematic components connected with fog. The Takoubelt, a stately dance, unfurls within the sight of hidden hills, the fog going about as an otherworldly shroud that isolates the holy from the commonplace.

In the Takoubelt, the musical thumps of drums reverberation through fog loaded scenes, and the ululations of the travelers penetrate the quietness of the desert air. The whirling dance of hidden figures turns into a demonstration of social respect to the cryptic fogs that effortlessness the Sahara. At these times, the fog isn't just a climatic event yet a member in a profound exchange that interfaces the Tuareg to the concealed elements of their roaming presence.

Rock Etchings: Roaming Accounts Carved in Stone

The roaming societies of the Sahara have left their stories carved in the very stones that take the stand concerning the progression of time. Rock etchings, dissipated across the desert, act as quiet narrators of itinerant life and their perplexing connection with the fog loaded domains. Tassili n'Ajjer, an UNESCO World Legacy site in Algeria, is one such vault of migrant stories cut into the rough material.

The etchings at Tassili n'Ajjer catch the dance of fog through the ages, deifying the migrant experiences with hidden ridges and air secrets.

Wanderers, portrayed in powerful scenes, explore fog loaded scenes, participate in formal practices, and cooperative with the concealed powers that saturate the desert air. These stone inscriptions stand as a demonstration of the getting through association between itinerant societies and the magical scenes they call home.

Transient Speculative chemistry: Fog and Topographical Stories

Roaming societies, well established in the Sahara's old scenes, have a significant appreciation for the topographical stories uncovered through fog. The fog, in its sensitive hug with the desert, turns into a fleeting revealer — a medium through which wanderers associate with the profound history recorded in the stones and developments.

The Hoggar Piles of Algeria, with their old stone craftsmanship and endured scenes, offer a material where fog discloses the topographical embroidery with newly discovered clearness. Travelers navigating the Hoggar Mountains wind up amidst a fleeting speculative chemistry, where fog relax the edges of time, uncovering rock developments as quiet sentinels that take the stand concerning centuries of land processes.

Traveling stories, shared around desert pit fires, frequently mesh the fog into the topographical texture of the Sahara. The stones, endured by wind and sand, become narrators, sharing the insider facts of the desert's profound history with each passing traveling age.

Social Strength: Migrant Transformations in Fog Loaded Domains

Roaming societies, formed by the unforgiving real factors of the desert, typify a strength manufactured through variation. Fog, with its irregular presence in bone-dry scenes, turns into an impetus for roaming variations, impacting everything from everyday schedules to social practices.

Water, a valuable item in the desert, takes on new importance in fog loaded domains. Wanderers, receptive to the nuances of the environment, may set up camps decisively to catch the dampness conveyed by fog. This versatile way to deal with water obtaining exhibits the harmonious connection between roaming societies and the vaporous climatic peculiarities that support life in the desert.

In fog loaded domains, itinerant networks might participate in transhumance, moving their crowds because of the accessibility of touching open doors impacted by a periodic dampness presented by fog. This portable way of life, synchronized with the regular rhythms of the desert, represents the social flexibility implanted in migrant variations.

Orchestra of the Faculties: Traveling Experiences with Fog

Traveling life in fog loaded deserts connects with the faculties in an orchestra of discernment that rises above the visual scene.

The hint of fog on the skin, an unobtrusive stroke challenging the dry assumptions for the Sahara, adds a layer of intricacy to the roaming experience. Migrants, hung in indigo robes and turbaned against the sun, feel the wet breath of fog amidst a climate familiar with dry breezes and singing intensity.

As fog plunges upon the ridges, it changes the soundscape of the Sahara. The typically quieted murmurs of the desert are adorned with the delicate mumble of dampness loaded air, making an environmental quiet that intensifies the isolation of the ridges. Travelers, receptive to the nuances of the desert's sounds, track down a melodic reverberation in the fog — a characteristic piece that blends with the old rhythms of their itinerant way of life.

Besides, the scent of fog, an uncommon olfactory extravagance in the parched field, adds a tactile layer to the Sahara's vibe. The fragrance of moist sand, blending with the natural smells of desert verdure, makes an olfactory orchestra that waits in the air. Wanderers, acclimated with the dry scent of the desert, experience a passing bouquet that goes with them through fog loaded hills, enhancing their tactile association with the Sahara.

Itinerant Folklore: Fog as a Scaffold Between Domains

Migrant societies, saturated with folklore and legends, frequently portray fog as a scaffold between the substantial and the profound domains. The Sahara's fogs, veiling the rises in ethereal magnificence, become entrances to aspects where spirits and divinities live. Migrant folklores mesh fog into the cosmological texture of the Sahara, changing it from a simple barometrical peculiarity into a course that interfaces the natural and the heavenly.

For the Tuareg, fog is an image of the concealed powers that impact their migrant presence. In the legends went down through ages, fog loaded rises are limits where travelers might experience otherworldly creatures, djinn, and tribal spirits. The moving sands, wrapped in fog, become a liminal space where the limits between the noticeable and the secret haze — a demonstration of the itinerant confidence in the otherworldly characteristics of their desert home.

Protection Contemplations: Supporting Migrant Customs and Fog Loaded Environments

As roaming societies keep on exploring fog loaded domains, protection endeavors should recognize and sustain the multifaceted connection between these societies and the environments formed by infrequent dampness. The supportability of roaming customs, complicatedly woven into the texture of fog loaded deserts, requires an all encompassing methodology that thinks about both social and natural elements.

Roaming transformations to fog, including water obtaining techniques and transhumance rehearses, ought to be incorporated into protection systems. Perceiving the harmonious connection between roaming societies and the biological systems impacted by fog becomes basic for economical land the executives in the desert.

Protection drives ought to endeavor to include itinerant networks as dynamic stewards of fog loaded scenes, guaranteeing that their customary information and practices add to the conservation of these delicate environments.

Furthermore, the vaporous idea of fog and its effect on desert biodiversity ought to be fundamental to protection contemplations. Desert gardens, supported by a periodic dampness presented by fog, are fundamental environments that help different verdure. Preservation systems should focus on the security of these fog supported desert springs as safe houses of biodiversity, recognizing their importance in supporting life in the bone-dry span of migrant regions.

Migrant Reverberations Through Fog Loaded Sands

As roaming societies proceed with their immortal hit the dance floor with the confounding fogs of deserts, their accounts reverberation through the fog loaded sands — a demonstration of the flexibility, versatility, and otherworldly extravagance woven into the embroidery of their reality. Itinerant stories, carved in stone, described around pit fires, and typified in ceremonial moves, divulge a profound association with the fog that shroud their traveling domains.

The itinerant relationship with desert fogs rises above the meteorological, wandering into the domains of otherworldliness, folklore, and social progression. Fog turns into a directing power, a buddy in the quiet excursion across rises, and a scaffold to concealed aspects. Roaming transformations to fog, from wayfinding abilities to water-obtaining methodologies, exhibit the unique exchange among people and the vaporous climatic peculiarities that shape their scenes.

In the protection of fog loaded environments, the safeguarding of migrant customs becomes fundamental. Roaming societies, with their profound comprehension of the desert's rhythms, are overseers of information that can add to maintainable land the board and the assurance of fog supported biodiversity. The sensitive harmony between migrant flexibility and fog loaded conditions highlights the requirement for protection drives that recognize and respect the multifaceted dance among people and the supernatural cover of the desert. In the reverberations of traveling stories through fog loaded sands, we track down a significant indication of the interconnectedness between societies, scenes, and the fleeting excellence that graces the deserts they call home.

Chapter 5

Frozen Whispers
Arctic Mist in Scandinavia

Frozen Murmurs: Icy Fog in Scandinavia

In the tremendous field of Scandinavia, where the Cold scene unfurls in an ensemble of ice and snow, a peculiarity both ethereal and magical graces the locale — the Icy fog. Not at all like the mild fogs that dance through lavish scenes, Icy fog is a frozen artful dance, a sensitive interaction between freezing temperatures and the dormant dampness that covers this northern domain. As we dive into the Icy fog of Scandinavia, we uncover a story woven with frigid strings, where murmurs of chilly air invoke an existence where reality and charm merge.

The Icy Expressive dance: Disclosing the Dance of Frozen Particles

In Scandinavia, particularly in the northern compasses of Norway, Sweden, and Finland, the Icy fog discloses itself as an artful dance of frozen particles suspended in the bone chilling air. It is a display brought into the world from the juxtaposition of frigid temperatures and the idle dampness of the Icy air. As the air becomes weighed down with translucent particles, a cover of fog emerges, changing the scene into a cold dreamscape.

In this Icy artful dance, the fog is definitely not a delicate three step dance yet a frozen pirouette — an expressive dance where every molecule is a transient artist spinning in the frigid virus. The Cold fog, as it unfurls across the frosty territory, cloak the scene in a gossamer cover, obscuring the limits among earth and sky. The frozen particles get the weak light of the Cold sun, making an unearthly feel where reality takes on a fanciful quality.

Lapland's Children's song: Icy Fog in Northern Finland

In the northern scopes of Finland, Lapland arises as a domain where the Icy fog coordinates a quiet cradlesong. Here, where snow-clad woodlands and frozen lakes characterize the scene, the fog adds a layer of charm to the colder time of year scene. Lapland's fog is definitely not a transient guest however an inhabitant craftsman, chiseling cold ponders that dazzle the creative mind.

As the fog plummets upon Lapland, it changes the coniferous timberlands into a domain of supernatural magnificence. The trees, covered in hoarfrost, stand as sentinels enveloped by a brilliant shroud. The fog, frozen midair, waits like a ghastly breath, making an air where time appears to be suspended. Lapland turns into a material where the Cold fog paints complicated examples of ice and ice, transforming the ordinary into the mystical.

Norwegian Fjords: Foggy Shroud Along Cold Shores

Along the sensational fjords of Norway, where tough bluffs dive into frigid waters, the Icy fog expects an oceanic person. Here, fog ascends from the bone chilling oceans, covering the waterfront scenes in shroud of frozen murmurs. The fjords, cut by old ice sheets, become theaters where fog and water take part in a ghastly dance.

The Norwegian Icy fog, affected by the vicinity of the ocean, winds through the fjords with an ethereal elegance. It embraces the lofty precipices, covering their glory in a puzzling hug. The fog, conveying the substance of the Icy waters, bestows a saline tang to the frozen air, making a tactile orchestra that rises above the visual display. Along the fjords, where the fog encompasses everything in a quieted quietude, the Cold scene unfurls as a show-stopper of nature's frigid masterfulness.

Winter Murmurs: Sweden's Subarctic Spell

In the subarctic scenes of Sweden, especially in districts like Swedish Lapland, the Icy fog enchants that changes the colder time of year view into a domain of frozen murmurs. As temperatures fall, the fog winds through snow-shrouded scenes, bringing about a charming interaction among ice and fleeting particles.

The subarctic fog in Sweden, similar to an otherworldly narrator, envelops the woodlands and fields by shroud of frozen stories. It sticks to branches, changing them into sensitive figures decorated with cold gems.

In this subarctic spell, the fog becomes both a craftsman and a chemist, transforming the commonplace into the uncommon. As the scene wears the ethereal clothing created by the Cold fog, Sweden's subarctic domains welcome thought and bring out a feeling of marvel.

Icy Nightfall: The Play of Light in Scandinavia's Colder time of year Skies

One of the most entrancing parts of the Cold fog in Scandinavia is its collaboration with the colder time of year skies during the polar evening. In the northernmost districts, the sun scarcely transcends the skyline during winter, projecting the scene into a delayed nightfall. The Cold fog, trapped in the hug of never-ending nightfall, turns into a material for the play of light and shadows.

As light waits on the cusp of haziness, the Cold fog changes the skies into a material of quieted tones. The diffused light communicates with frozen particles, making a peculiarity known as "Icy nightfall." The scene, washed in this extraordinary heavenly shine, takes on a supernatural appearance. The fog, frozen in time, turns into a course for the fragile dance between the decreasing light and the arising stars — an exhibition that rises above the limits of the regular and the powerful.

Itinerant Reverberations: Sámi Culture and the Cold Fog

In the Icy fog loaded scenes of Scandinavia, the Sámi public, native to the locale, have developed a profound association with their frigid environmental factors. The Sámi, generally roaming reindeer herders, explore the frozen tundra with a cozy information on the Cold fog's rhythms and subtleties. As far as they might be concerned, fog isn't simply a climatic event however a sidekick in their migrant presence.

Sámi culture, rich with customs and otherworldliness, entwines with the Icy fog in manners that mirror an agreeable concurrence with nature. The Sámi, frequently connected with energetic conventional dressing enhanced with mind boggling designs, move nimbly through fog loaded scenes. Their reindeer crowds, adjusted to the Cold circumstances, brush in the ethereal cloak of ice, making a harmonious scene where migrant life and fog unite.

Auroras and Cold Speculative chemistry: Heavenly Artful dance in Scandinavia

The Icy fog, with its frozen particles suspended in the air, turns into a vital player in the heavenly artful dance that graces the Cold skies — Aurora Borealis, or auroras. In Scandinavia, where the Cold fog blends with the charged particles from the sun, the night sky changes into a material where iridescent greens, purples, and pinks dance in a vast showcase.

The connection between the Cold fog and the auroras makes a peculiarity likened to heavenly speculative chemistry. The frozen particles in the fog go about as a crystal, refracting the illumination of the auroras in hypnotizing designs. The Icy fog turns into a cloak through which Aurora Borealis weave their heavenly stories, providing reason to feel ambiguous about a charm the Icy scenes.

For those lucky enough to observe this heavenly artful dance in Scandinavia, the Cold fog turns into an assistant in the dance of light and shadow that paints the colder time of year skies.

Preservation and Icy Delicacy: Supporting the Frozen Environments

As Scandinavia's Cold fog proceeds to charm and enamor, the delicacy of this frozen biological system comes into sharp concentration. Protection endeavors in the Cold locales should perceive the mind boggling dance among fog and scene and endeavor to save the fragile equilibrium that supports this stormy wonderland.

The Icy fog, entwined with the more extensive Icy environments, assumes a part in keeping up with the soundness of frozen scenes. As temperatures vacillate, the fog adds to the arrangement of ice gems and ice, affecting the elements of snowpack and supporting the flexibility of Icy greenery. Preservation systems should focus on the security of these fog loaded conditions, recognizing their significance in supporting life in outrageous circumstances.

Besides, the Cold fog is a sentinel of environmental change, with modifications in temperature and air conditions influencing its development and conduct. As the Cold area goes through quick changes, protection drives should be proactive in tending to the effects on fog loaded scenes. Observing and research endeavors ought to be escalated to grasp the subtleties of fog development in the changing Icy environment, empowering informed preservation choices.

Frozen Verse in Cold Fog

In the stormy domains of Scandinavia, the Icy fog unfurls as a graceful orchestra, where frozen particles dance in the virus embrace of northern scenes. From Lapland's captivated woodlands to the fog covered fjords of Norway, every locale adds to the aggregate story of Cold fog, making a mosaic of frozen verse.

The Cold fog, with its fragile touch and ethereal presence, changes Scandinavia into a domain where reality and charm mix. A peculiarity rises above meteorology, turning into a necessary piece of social, profound, and natural stories. As the Cold fog murmurs through frozen scenes, it welcomes examination, wonderment, and a profound appreciation for the delicate magnificence that graces the northern scopes of our planet. In the frozen murmurs of Icy fog, Scandinavia uncovers itself as a domain where nature's verse is written in glasslike stanzas, welcoming all who witness it to turn out to be important for the immortal dance among fog and ice in the Cold territory.

5.1 Navigating the chilling beauty of mist in Scandinavia.

Exploring the Chilling Magnificence of Fog in Scandinavia: A Stormy Odyssey

Scandinavia, a land where the great meets the obvious, is supplied with a chilling delight that unfurls in the fragile hug of fog. This snowy odyssey, where the scenes are decorated in layers of ice and hidden in ethereal wisps, coaxes bold travelers into an existence where reality and charm merge. Exploring the chilling magnificence of fog in Scandinavia is an excursion through domains where frozen murmurs and cold embroidered works of art make a climatic orchestra that resounds with the quintessence of the North.

Cold Cover: An Ensemble of Fog and Ice

In Scandinavia's Icy spans, fog turns into a natural power, coordinating an ensemble of ice and environmental speculative chemistry. The Icy shroud, woven by fog in a joint effort with freezing temperatures, wrap the scene in frozen verse. As one endeavors into the tremendous tundra and snow-covered scopes, the fog changes the landscape into a dreamscape where the limits among earth and sky obscure.

The chilling excellence of fog in Scandinavia is especially articulated during the polar evening, when light melts away, and the scene is shrouded in ceaseless nightfall. In this divine artful dance, fog accepts an ethereal gleam, getting the muffled light of the Cold sun. The outcome is a fragile interchange of shadows and glow, where the scene shows up as though it were painted by the brushstrokes of winter itself.

Winter's Murmur: Supernatural Experiences in Nordic Timberlands

Exploring the fog loaded backwoods of Scandinavia during winter is an excursion into the core of Nordic mystery. The trees, decorated with hoarfrost, stand sentinel in the frozen quiet, and the backwoods floor turns into a rug of sensitive gems. As the fog winds through the trees, it makes a feeling of powerful nature — a domain where the commonplace is changed into the exceptional.

In these otherworldly experiences, the chilling excellence of fog uncovers itself in the transaction of light and shadow. The fog, frozen into small particles, refracts the encompassing light, providing reason to feel ambiguous about an ethereal shine the Nordic woodlands. It is a play of Winter's murmurs, where the scene turns into a residing sonnet, and each step is a verse in the quiet tribute to the excellence of the North.

Lapland's Spell: Cold Fog in the Northern Spans

Lapland, the northernmost district of Finland, is a domain where the Cold fog does magic, changing the scene into a colder time of year wonderland. As one endeavors into Lapland's huge wild, the fog becomes both a craftsman and a conjurer. It cover the fells and waterways in a transparent cover, transforming the recognizable into the uncommon.

Exploring Lapland's Icy fog is a concentrate in contrasts. The fog, with its frozen breath, adds a fleeting quality to the scene, while the evergreen trees, decorated with ice, stand as getting through sentinels against the chill. The frozen waterways, winding through the dim landscape, become pathways to the obscure — an excursion into the core of Lapland's stormy charm.

Fjords in Cover: Enchanted Oceanic Fogs in Norway

Along Norway's sensational fjords, fog assumes a sea personality, veiling the waterfront scenes in mysterious covers. The fjords, cut by old icy masses, become theaters where fog and water take part in a ghostly dance. Exploring these fog loaded fjords is a sea odyssey where the components scheme to make a visual ensemble.

The chilling magnificence of fog in Norway's fjords is elevated by the tough bluffs that dive into frigid waters. The fog, ascending from the cold oceans, sticks to the precipices, changing them into transcending apparitions hung in ethereal cover. As one sails through the fog covered fjords, the sea air becomes accused of a feeling of secret and wonderment, as though each curve in the fjord holds a mystery ready to be revealed.

Subarctic Quietness: Sweden's Ethereal Scenes

Wandering into the subarctic scenes of Sweden, especially in areas like Swedish Lapland, is a submersion into the peacefulness of chilling magnificence. The Cold fog, here, assumes a subarctic personality, making scenes that are both tormenting and peaceful. Exploring the fog loaded domains of subarctic Sweden is an excursion into an ethereal wild, where the land appears to inhale with the sensitive bit of ice.

In these subarctic scenes, the chilling magnificence of fog appears in the unobtrusive exchange between frozen particles and the fragile elements of the land. The fog, frozen in midair, refracts the curbed light of the colder time of year sun, making a delicate radiance that washes the scene in a peaceful shine. Sweden's subarctic domains welcome contemplation, offering a material where fog and isolation mix into a visual verse of frozen serenity.

Social Reverberation: Exploring Fog in Sámi Domains

The chilling magnificence of fog in Scandinavia isn't just a visual exhibition yet additionally a social reverberation, particularly in the domains possessed by the Sámi public. Exploring fog in Sámi domains is an excursion into a social scene where fog isn't just a meteorological peculiarity yet a friend in the itinerant presence of these native individuals.

For the Sámi, fog turns into an essential piece of their social character. The Sámi culture, profoundly entwined with nature, recognizes the chilling magnificence of fog as an otherworldly and air presence. Exploring the fog loaded scenes in Sámi regions offers looks into a perspective where the limits between the unmistakable and the otherworldly are obscured —

a social embroidery where fog turns into an emblematic string associating the Sámi nation to their Icy country.

Heavenly Expressive dance: Aurora's Dance in Hazy Skies

In the chilling magnificence of fog loaded skies, Scandinavia presents a divine expressive dance where fog and Aurora Borealis play out an ethereal dance. Exploring dim skies during the polar night turns into an odyssey into an enormous scene where the radiant shades of the auroras communicate with the frozen particles suspended in the air.

As fog shroud the heavenly material, Aurora Borealis take on a one of a kind quality. The fog, refracting the grandiose gleam, adds a diffused splendor to the auroras, making an environmental speculative chemistry that rises above the limits among earth and space. Exploring this divine expressive dance in Scandinavia is an experience with the grand, as fog and auroras join to paint the frigid night sky with strokes of enormous charm.

Preservation in the Fog Loaded North: Adjusting Delicacy

As Scandinavia's fog loaded scenes dazzle the creative mind, the delicacy of these environments becomes obvious. Protection endeavors in the fog loaded North should adjust the safeguarding of chilling magnificence with the sensitive complexities of Cold environments. The fog, as a unique power in these scenes, assumes an imperative part in keeping up with the strength of frozen conditions.

Saving fog loaded biological systems requires a nuanced approach that thinks about the exchange between fog, temperature, and scene highlights. Protection methodologies should perceive the significance of fog in supporting Cold widely varied vegetation, adding to the arrangement of ice gems and ice that shape the environmental elements. Adjusting delicacy includes figuring out the job of fog in the more extensive Cold setting and creating preservation drives that shield these sensitive environments.

In addition, as the Icy area goes through fast environmental change, protection endeavors should be versatile and proactive. Observing the effect of changing climatic circumstances on fog development and conduct becomes basic for informed protection choices. The delicacy of fog loaded environments requires a promise to saving the chilling excellence of the North while tending to the difficulties presented by a warming environment.

A Chilly Dream in Fog Loaded Domains

Exploring the chilling magnificence of fog in Scandinavia is an excursion into domains where cold dream and snowy charm entwine. From the Cold tundra to fog covered fjords, each scene adds to a visual ensemble that reverberates with the quintessence of the North. Fog, frozen in sensitive ballet performances, turns into a friend in this frigid odyssey, welcoming investigation and thought.

In the chilling magnificence of fog loaded domains, Scandinavia uncovers itself as a land where nature's nuances and loftiness merge.

The fragile hint of fog, refracting the surrounding light, changes the scene into a material where reality and charm blend. Exploring fog in the North is in excess of an actual excursion — it is a drenching into social reverberation, heavenly ballet productions, and the delicate magnificence of Cold biological systems.

As we explore the fog loaded magnificence of Scandinavia, we become members in a cold dream, where each experience with fog divulges another feature of the North's snowy charm. In the quiet of fog loaded backwoods, the dance of Aurora Borealis, and the migrant reverberations of Sámi domains, Scandinavia welcomes us to investigate the chilling excellence that characterizes its fog loaded domains — a stunner that waits in the creative mind long after the cold odyssey reaches a conclusion.

5.2 Examining mist's role in the unique ecosystems of the Arctic Circle.

Looking at Fog's Job in the Remarkable Biological systems of the Icy Circle: A Shroud of Delicacy in a Frozen Domain

The Cold Circle, an immense and freezing field enclosing the polar district, is home to environments formed by limits. In this frozen domain, fog arises as an unobtrusive yet powerful player, winding around its fleeting strings through the mind boggling embroidery of Cold scenes. Looking at fog's part in the one of a kind biological systems of the Cold Circle uncovers a sensitive shroud of delicacy that adds subtlety to the power of life in this outrageous climate.

An Ensemble of Ice Gems: Fog as Engineer of Icy Ice

In the Cold Circle, where temperatures plunge and the air is weighed down with dampness, fog turns into the draftsman of Icy ice. This peculiarity, frequently alluded to as ice haze, happens when fog particles suspended in the air freeze upon contact with surfaces, changing scenes into ethereal domains of glasslike magnificence. Looking at the job of fog in the development of Icy ice uncovers an orchestra of ice precious stones that embellishes everything from vegetation to the very air itself.

Fog loaded biological systems in the Cold Circle are unpredictably associated with the development of ice designs on surfaces. As fog particles freeze, they make sensitive ice feathers, unpredictable greenery like designs, and delicate shroud that wrap over vegetation. The job of fog in this cycle isn't just meteorological; it is a stone worker, forming the Cold scene into a transient magnum opus of frozen multifaceted design.

Fog Supported Desert gardens: Supporting Icy Vegetation in Outrageous Circumstances

Analyzing the job of fog in the Icy Circle goes past the visual display of ice designs; it digs into the food of Cold vegetation in conditions that are brutal and outrageous.

Fog, with its idle dampness, supports microhabitats that act as desert springs for vegetation. These fog supported desert springs become fundamental pockets of biodiversity in a scene where each asset is scant.

The Cold tundra, with its low temperatures and short developing season, depends on the dampness presented by fog for the endurance of plant species. Greeneries, lichens, and low-lying vascular plants, adjusted to the Icy's cruel circumstances, draw food from the fog loaded air. Looking at fog's job as a supplier of dampness in these biological systems highlights its importance as a nurturing force, cultivating biodiversity amidst a generally somber climate.

Roaming Route: Sámi Reindeer Grouping and Fog's Direction

Inside the Icy Circle, fog turns into an aide for migrant networks, outstandingly the Sámi nation who practice reindeer grouping. The fog loaded scenes act as a setting for traveling route, where the climatic circumstances are not simply meteorological yet essential to the roaming lifestyle. Looking at fog with regards to Sámi reindeer crowding divulges a social beneficial interaction with Icy climates.

For the Sámi, fog goes about as a characteristic aide during relocations. The frozen particles in the fog make unobtrusive prompts that guide in wayfinding across the tremendous tundra. The sodden air, frequently shaping fog loaded cloak, turns into a navigational partner for the Sámi as they cross the Cold scenes. Inspecting this multifaceted connection among fog and traveling route features how barometrical circumstances are woven into the texture of social works on, changing fog from a climatic event to a social sidekick.

Icy Sundown Speculative chemistry: Fog's Commitment to Divine Showcases

In the Icy Circle, where polar evenings cast delayed nightfalls, fog adds to the speculative chemistry of heavenly presentations. Looking at fog's job in the Icy dusk uncovers how the sensitive exchange between fog particles and encompassing light improves the visual scene of Aurora Borealis, or auroras. Fog turns into a refractive medium that adds subtlety to the grandiose expressive dance unfurling in the Cold skies.

As fog cloak the divine material, Aurora Borealis take on a delicate, diffused gleam. The fog particles refract the astronomical light, making mind boggling designs that dance across the frozen region. Looking at fog's commitment to divine presentations highlights its job in molding earthbound scenes as well as in adding a bit of ethereal sorcery to the Icy evenings. Fog, in this unique situation, turns into a partner in the heavenly venue that charms eyewitnesses sufficiently lucky to observe the Cold nightfall.

Saving Icy Delicacy: Perceiving Fog's Weakness

Looking at fog's job in the remarkable biological systems of the Icy Circle requires a more profound comprehension of the delicacy of fog loaded conditions.

Fog, while adding to the magnificence and usefulness of Cold scenes, is likewise powerless against changes in environment and climatic circumstances. Preservation endeavors should perceive fog's weakness and address the more extensive difficulties looked by the Cold Circle in a warming world.

The delicacy of fog loaded biological systems lies in their aversion to temperature varieties. As the Icy encounters fast environmental change, adjustments in temperature and barometrical circumstances can affect fog development and conduct. Preservation techniques should be versatile, considering the fragile harmony between fog, ice, and the general strength of Icy biological systems. Inspecting fog's weakness turns into a source of inspiration, encouraging traditionalists to protect the scenes molded by fog as well as the climatic circumstances that support this sensitive barometrical peculiarity.

Cold Insight: Native Points of view on Fog's Quintessence

Looking at fog's job in the extraordinary biological systems of the Icy Circle stretches out past logical request; it embraces native points of view that view fog as in excess of a climatic event. Native people group inside the Icy Circle have a significant insight that perceives fog's substance as a social, otherworldly, and biological power. Looking at fog from native perspectives uncovers a comprehensive comprehension that rises above logical order.

Native points of view feature fog as a unique presence that impacts the visual feel of the scene as well as the profound and social elements of Cold life. Fog, in these viewpoints, turns into a conductor between the unmistakable and the immaterial — a peculiarity that associates the seen and the concealed. Looking at fog's substance through native insight welcomes a change in worldview, recognizing the interconnectedness of fog with the more extensive Cold story.

Frozen Ecotones: Looking at Fog's Impact on Icy Limits

In the Icy Circle, where environments progress between tundra, boreal timberland, and polar desert, fog goes about as an unobtrusive orchestrator of ecotones. Inspecting fog's effect on Icy limits uncovers how this climatic peculiarity adds to the formation of temporary zones that harbor exceptional biodiversity. Fog, with its capacity to obscure environmental limits, turns into an impetus for the development of different and strong biological systems.

The fog loaded air, wealthy in dampness, assumes a vital part in forming the ecotones of the Icy Circle. These temporary zones, where fog communicates with assorted scenes, become asylums for particular verdure. Looking at fog's effect on Cold limits underlines the requirement for preservation endeavors that perceive the significance of ecotones in supporting biodiversity in an evolving environment. Fog, as an unpretentious engineer of limits, turns into a central participant in keeping up with the flexibility and versatility of Icy biological systems.

A Fragile Embroidery Woven in Icy Fog

Looking at fog's job in the extraordinary environments of the Icy Circle uncovers a fragile embroidery woven in frozen strings. From the engineering style of Cold ice to the itinerant route directed by fog, every perspective adds to the flexibility and magnificence of Icy scenes. Fog, in its nuance and weakness, arises as a power that rises above the limits between science, culture, and biology.

As we dive into the complex exchange among fog and Cold biological systems, a story unfurls — one that welcomes us to perceive the delicacy of fog loaded conditions and the insight implanted in native viewpoints. Inspecting fog turns into an excursion into domains where environmental peculiarities shape the actual parts of the scene as well as the social and profound elements of Icy life.

Fog in the Cold Circle is in excess of a meteorological event; it is a buddy in the frozen odyssey of life. Perceiving fog's part in the remarkable environments of the Cold Circle prompts us to move toward protection with a comprehensive grasping that embraces the interconnectedness of barometrical peculiarities with the different features of Icy presence. Fog, as it cover the Cold scenes in sensitive tastefulness, welcomes us to examine the complexities of this frozen domain — a domain where fog turns into an ethereal narrator, murmuring stories of versatility, flexibility, and the persevering through magnificence of the Icy Circle.

5.3 Tales of northern lights and misty fjords.

Stories of Aurora Borealis and Dim Fjords: An Orchestra in the Cold Evening

In the furthest reaches of the Northern Side of the equator, where the polar breezes murmur through snow-clad scenes, stories unfurl that are scratched in the heavenly material of the Icy evening. Among these stories, the entwining stories of Aurora Borealis and dim fjords make an ensemble of ethereal excellence that enamors the creative mind and reverberates with the soul of the Cold. These are stories that rise above the limits of legends, winding around a story where the glowing dance of the auroras blends with the tricky cloak of fog, laying out a scene that is on the double hauntingly otherworldly and significantly baffling.

Auroras: Divine Movement in Icy Skies

Aurora Borealis, or auroras, are divine peculiarities that effortlessness the polar skies with an extraordinary artful dance of varieties. These glowing presentations, prevalently found in the high-scope locales close to the Cold Circle, are the consequence of charged particles from the sun slamming into climatic gases. In the Icy evening, the stories of auroras unfurl as lively draperies of green, pink, and violet, making a steadily moving display that challenges natural examinations.

As the sun sets beneath the skyline during the polar evening, the stage is set for the divine movement of the auroras. Stories of Aurora Borealis are entwined with the mysterious characteristics of fog, as the glowing bends and twirls become ethereal brushstrokes on the material of the Cold evening. The fog loaded air adds a diffused quality to the divine gleam, changing the auroras into a heavenly artful dance that appears to move as one with the cover of fog beneath.

Hazy Fjords: Cover of Secret Along Icy Shores

While Aurora Borealis paint the sky with their heavenly shades, the dim fjords of the Icy shores underneath contribute their own stories of secret and charm. Fjords, cut by antiquated ice sheets, are profound, slender channels flanked by transcending bluffs that dive into frigid waters. As fog ascends from the cold oceans, these fjords become hidden in ethereal covers, making an air of interest and persona.

The stories of cloudy fjords are stories of hidden glory — where rough scenes are somewhat covered, welcoming the creative mind to fill in the holes. As the fog winds through the fjords, it changes the transcending bluffs into ghostly outlines, delivering the recognizable scenes into some-thing practically extraordinary. Stories of foggy fjords reverberation with the sound of lapping waters and the unpleasant calls of seabirds, making a tangible encounter that rises above the visual, drenching the people who adventure into this fog loaded domain in a dreamscape of Icy miracle.

Heavenly Agreement: Auroras and Fog's Fragile Dance

In the Cold evening, stories of Aurora Borealis and cloudy fjords unite in a heavenly concordance, where the radiant dance of the auroras tracks down a sensitive accomplice in the slippery hug of fog. As the auroras cast their divine shine across the sky, fog ascends from the fjords, making a visual ensemble that lifts the Icy scene to a domain of unmatched excellence.

The heavenly dance unfurls as fog cover the fjords, making a delicate differentiation to the striking shades of the auroras. The ethereal shine of

Aurora Borealis, refracted through the fog loaded air, takes on a muffled and diffused quality, transforming the Cold night into a material where light and shadow participate in a heavenly three step dance. These stories of heavenly concordance are not simply visual; they are an encouragement to encounter the Cold night as a multisensory magnum opus, where the interchange of fog and auroras makes an ensemble that resounds with the spirit.

Old stories and Folklore: The Spirits Behind the Cover

In the rich embroidery of Icy old stories and folklore, stories of Aurora Borealis and hazy fjords are woven with strings of profound importance. Native societies in the Icy have made accounts that quality the auroras to spirits and divine creatures. The fog, as well, is many times considered a domain where spirits stay, and the shroud of fog are viewed as limits to powerful aspects.

In these stories, Aurora Borealis are once in a while accepted to be the dance of genealogical spirits, winding around stories in the vast embroidery. The fog, ascending from the fjords, turns into a medium through which spirits cross between the natural and the profound domains. Stories of dim fjords and auroras in Icy fables bring out a feeling of veneration for the normal world, where the heavenly and the earthbound are entwined, and the limits between the seen and the concealed are obscured.

An Excursion into the Icy Evening: Mysterious Experiences

For the people who set out on an excursion into the Icy evening, stories of Aurora Borealis and foggy fjords become solicitations to mysterious experiences. Directed by the brilliant bends of the auroras and tricked by the shroud of fog along the fjords, explorers wind up drenched in a domain that rises above the common. The Icy evening, with its stories of heavenly marvels and hazy charm, turns into a material for individual stories of stunningness and miracle.

As voyagers explore the cloudy fjords, the play of light and shadow, combined with the divine dance above, makes an environment of strange magnificence. The stories brought into the world from these experiences are tied in with seeing normal peculiarities as well as about turning out to be important for the narratives written in the Cold evening. Whether it's the quiet of fog loaded fjords or the lively tones of Aurora Borealis, each experience turns into a section in an individual story — an excursion into the core of the Icy's persona.

Environmental Concordance: Fog and Fjords as Biological system Impetuses

Past the stories of magnificence and charm, the dim fjords assume an imperative part in the natural congruity of the Cold. The fog loaded air, wealthy in dampness, adds to the fragile equilibrium of waterfront biological systems. Fjords become impetuses for supplement cycling and marine life, supporting a different exhibit of animal categories that are complicatedly associated with the foggy domains.

The stories of fog and fjords reach out to the environmental accounts of the Cold, where supplement rich waters cultivate flourishing marine biological systems. Fog, as it ascends from the freezing oceans and blends with waterfront scenes, turns into a wellspring of essentialness for the complicated snare of life. The fjords, cut by old icy masses and supported in fog, are scenes of stylish charm as well as centers of natural interconnectedness, where fog and fjords team up to support life in the cruelest of conditions.

Monitoring the Cold Persona: Saving Stories for Ages

As stories of Aurora Borealis and hazy fjords keep on dazzling hearts and psyches, the requirement for preservation becomes vital. Saving the Cold persona, with its divine ponders and fog loaded scenes, isn't simply an ecological basic however a promise to protecting the rich social and profound legacy implanted in these stories.

Preservation endeavors should perceive the delicacy of the Icy environments that bring about these stories. Aurora Borealis and foggy fjords are not simply grand marvels; they are signs of the wellbeing of the Cold climate. Protecting stories for people in the future includes feasible practices, mindful the travel industry, and a profound regard for the fragile equilibrium that supports the magnificence of the Cold evening.

Reverberations of Charm in the Icy Evening

In the Cold evening, where stories of Aurora Borealis and dim fjords unfurl, reverberations of charm wait in the air. These stories are not confined accounts; they are parts in a stupendous story composed essentially itself — a story that welcomes us to wonder about the heavenly expressive dance above and the dim cover beneath. Aurora Borealis, with their divine tints, dance as one with the fog, making an orchestra that rises above the common.

As we finish up our investigation of stories in the Icy evening, we end up remaining at the edge of a domain where excellence and secret mix. The reverberations of charm in the Icy night are not restricted to the pages of fables or the edges of photos; they are alive in the murmurs of fog loaded fjords and the heavenly dance of the auroras. The Cold evening, with its stories of Aurora Borealis and dim fjords, entices us to tune in, to observe, and to turn out to be essential for a story that rises above time — an account that unfurls in the radiant circular segments of Aurora Borealis and the slippery shroud of fog, winding around a story that will persevere in the aggregate creative mind for a long time into the future.

Chapter 6

Pacific Islands
Veiled Paradises

Pacific Islands: Hidden Heavens - Where Nature and Culture Meet
The Pacific Islands, dispersed across the huge territory of the Pacific Sea, structure an embroidery of hidden heavens, where nature and culture combine in agreeable wonder. This archipelagic domain, known for its sky blue waters, lavish scenes, and lively coral reefs, entices voyagers into an existence where the limits between natural excellence and social extravagance obscure. In investigating the Pacific Islands, one sets out on an excursion into hidden heavens that uncover stories of versatility, social legacy, and the fragile dance among humanity and the normal world.

Lavish Scenes: Nature's Shroud Across the Islands
The Pacific Islands, eminent for their lavish scenes, are hung in a characteristic cloak that spellbinds the faculties. From the emerald slopes of Hawaii to the thick rainforests of Papua New Guinea, every island adds to the account of hidden heavens. The lavishness of these scenes isn't simply a visual exhibition; it is an encouragement to drench oneself in the hug of nature's cover, where verdant foliage disguises stowed away ponders and dynamic biodiversity.

The stories of rich scenes in the Pacific Islands discuss a sensitive biological equilibrium. Rainforests, with their fog covered shelters, harbor endemic species found no place else on The planet. Coral reefs, covered underneath the sea's surface, overflow with life in a dynamic presentation of varieties. The hidden heavens of the Pacific Islands, with their biodiversity and normal wonder, highlight the significance of protection endeavors that save the fragile biological systems supporting these rich scenes.

Social Lavishness: Stories Woven in Customs

Past the regular charm, the Pacific Islands brag a social extravagance woven into the texture of their social orders. Every island is an embroidery of stories, customs, and customs that have persevered for ages. The social cover across the Pacific Islands uncovers stories of flexibility, familial insight, and a profound association between individuals and their surroundings.

In Polynesia, the specialty of route utilizing heavenly signs is a demonstration of the marine legacy of the islanders. In Melanesia, the multifaceted woodcarvings and energetic services are articulations of social character. Micronesia, with its decentralized social designs, tells stories of public concordance. The social wealth of the Pacific Islands is hidden in the customs of dance, the songs of customary music, and the lively shades of native craftsmanship. These social stories, woven into the islands' character, mirror the flexibility of networks that have explored the difficulties of time while saving their remarkable legacy.

Maritime Persona: Coral Reefs as Submerged Shroud

Underneath the cerulean waters that encompass the Pacific Islands lies a maritime persona — a complicated universe of coral reefs that fills in as a submerged cloak. The coral reefs, with their vivid cluster of marine life, are significant of the sensitive harmony among humanity and nature. Stories of the maritime persona disclose the difficulties looked by these biological systems and the continuous endeavors to safeguard the delicate submerged heavens.

Coral reefs, hidden underneath the surface, are imperative environments that help a heap of marine animal types. The energetic shades of coral developments diverge from the more profound blues of the untamed sea, making a visual exhibition that reflects the biodiversity flourishing inside. The stories of the maritime persona are, notwithstanding, touched with worry as environmental change and human exercises present dangers to these sensitive biological systems. Preservation drives across the Pacific Islands plan to disclose a feasible future for coral reefs, guaranteeing that the maritime persona perseveres for a long time into the future.

Island Containers: Exploring the Social Mosaic

Exploring the Pacific Islands is an excursion of island bouncing — an investigation of the different social mosaic that portrays the district. Every island, with its one of a kind practices and customs, adds to the rich embroidery of Pacific culture.

The specialty of island jumping turns into a vessel for explorers to disclose the subtleties of neighborhood life, from the cadenced thumps of conventional drumming in Samoa to the unpredictable tattoos of the Maori in New Zealand.

Island bouncing isn't simply an actual excursion; a social odyssey welcomes explorers to drench themselves in the day to day rhythms of island life. The stories of island containers unfurl in dynamic business sectors, where nearby craftsmans feature their artworks, and in public social occasions, where conventional moves and eats celebrate social variety. Through island jumping, explorers become observers to the flexibility of Pacific societies, uncovering the narratives scratched into the scenes and seascapes.

Evaporating Skylines: Environmental Change as an Uncovering Power

While the Pacific Islands are much of the time saw as hidden heavens, environmental change has arisen as an uncovering force, uncovering the weakness of these charming scenes. Rising ocean levels, outrageous climate occasions, and sea fermentation compromise the actual groundworks of the Pacific Islands. The stories of evaporating skylines mirror the critical requirement for worldwide mindfulness and aggregate activity to relieve the effects of environmental change on these weak archipelagos.

The islands of the Pacific are on the forefronts of environmental change, confronting difficulties that incorporate loss of land, disturbances to customary lifestyles, and dangers to biodiversity. As skylines disappear because of infringing waters, the Pacific Islands are at the front of supporting for environment equity and feasible practices. The uncovering power of environmental change constrains a reexamination of how mankind cooperates with the climate, encouraging a shift toward protection, environmentally friendly power, and mindful ecological stewardship.

Sacrosanct Destinations: Profound Shroud Across the Islands

Inside the Pacific Islands, hallowed destinations structure otherworldly shroud that interface individuals to the land, ocean, and sky. These locales, frequently covered in social importance and encompassed by lavish scenes, are storehouses of familial insight and sacrosanct accounts. The stories of sacrosanct destinations unfurl as journeys to these spots become excursions of respect, where guests and local people the same divulge the otherworldly substance implanted in the land.

From the volcanic pinnacles of Hawaii, where the highest points are viewed as hallowed domains, to the marae of Tahiti, where old stone sanctuaries stand as demonstrations of profound legacy, the Pacific Islands are permeated with holiness. These otherworldly cloak act as tokens of the characteristic association among culture and nature, directing the occupants in their communications with the climate. The stories of sacrosanct locales reveal an all encompassing perspective, where the material and otherworldly aspects are interwoven, cultivating a profound regard for the normal world.

Wayfinders of Versatility: Cruising Through Pacific Difficulties

The Pacific Islands are home to wayfinders — networks that explore the difficulties of innovation while saving their social and ecological legacy. The stories of wayfinders unfurl as accounts of versatility, where islanders adjust to changing conditions while remaining consistent with their underlying foundations. The difficulties of globalization, financial movements, and natural dangers are met with a feeling of development and a pledge to defending hidden heavens.

The wayfinders of the Pacific encapsulate a way of thinking that rises above simple endurance; it is a demonstration of flourishing notwithstanding misfortune. Through maintainable practices, social safeguarding, and local area commitment, these islanders reveal a way toward a strong future. The stories of wayfinders highlight the significance of native information, local area cooperation, and worldwide fortitude in tending to the remarkable difficulties looked by the Pacific Islands.

Preservation as Revealing: Safeguarding the Pacific Inheritance

Protection endeavors across the Pacific Islands act as a disclosing force, uncovering the devotion of networks and associations to defending the regular and social tradition of these heavens. Stories of preservation unfurl as drives center around safeguarding biodiversity, advancing feasible the travel industry, and tending to the effects of environmental change. From marine safeguarded regions to local area based projects, these endeavors intend to uncover a future where the Pacific Islands keep on flourishing.

Protecting the Pacific inheritance requires a comprehensive methodology that thinks about both the normal and social elements of these islands. Preservation turns into a cooperative undertaking that includes neighborhood networks, states, and worldwide organizations. The stories of protection are accounts of trust, versatility, and a common obligation to disclosing the potential for congruity among humanity and the climate.

Uncovering the Excellence Inside the Pacific Shroud

Our investigation of the Pacific Islands, it becomes apparent that these hidden heavens are not simply geological substances; they are vaults of stories, flexibility, and the fragile dance among nature and culture. The lavish scenes, social extravagance, maritime persona, and difficulties looked by the Pacific Islands add to a story that uncovers the complexities of life in this huge archipelagic domain.

The stories of the Pacific Islands welcome us to see the value in the magnificence inside the shroud — the sensitive harmony among nature and culture that characterizes these heavens. As we reveal the tales carved into the scenes, jump into the maritime persona, and witness the versatility of island networks, we track down a significant association with the Pacific inheritance.

These hidden heavens are not simply objections; they are living stories that rouse a pledge to protection, social conservation, and an amicable relationship with the normal world. The Pacific Islands, with their excellence both seen and concealed, stay a charming embroidery — a woven artwork that coaxes us to investigate, regard, and reveal the endless marvels inside the Pacific cover.

6.1 Embracing the tropical allure of mist in Pacific island destinations.

Embracing the Tropical Appeal of Fog in Pacific Island Locations: Hidden Excellence Revealed

In the core of the tremendous Pacific Sea, where turquoise waters support lavish archipelagos, a dazzling peculiarity winds around its charm — the tropical charm of fog. Pacific island locations, eminent for their paradisiacal scenes, are hidden in the ethereal excellence of fog, adding a layer of charm to the generally dazzling embroidery of these tropical domains. This investigation brings us into the core of fog loaded heavens, where the cover of tropical charm disguises stories of secret, biological extravagance, and the social meaning of fog in the Pacific.

Fog Wrapped Mountains: Magical Tops in Hawaii

Hawaii, an archipelago described by volcanic pinnacles ascending from the Pacific profundities, is many times covered in fog that loans a magical quality to its scenes. The stories of fog enclosed mountains by Hawaii unfurl as the volcanic pinnacles, as Mauna Kea and Mauna Loa, become hidden in sensitive mists. These fog loaded levels make an extraordinary scene, where the crossing point of volcanic powers and tropical air brings forth an enamoring dance of fog and light.

The fog in Hawaii serves as an air peculiarity as well as a social standard. In Hawaiian folklore, the fog is frequently connected with the presence of spirits, adding a layer of otherworldly importance to these fog wrapped mountains. The tropical charm of fog in Hawaii, with its puzzling shroud, hence turns into a scaffold between the substantial and the profound, welcoming voyagers to embrace the normal excellence as well as the social stories woven into the dim scenes.

Flowing Shroud: Cascade Style in Tahiti

As we cross the immensity of the Pacific, the tropical charm of fog takes us to Tahiti, where flowing cloak of fog cover magnificent cascades. The cascades of Tahiti, for example, the notorious Vaipoiri Falls, plunge through rich vegetation, making a charming showcase of fog kissed style. These fog loaded overflows, concealed inside the core of the island, bring out a feeling of tranquility and normal quality.

The stories of flowing shroud in Tahiti reverberation with the social meaning of water in Polynesian customs. Cascades, hidden in fog, are viewed as holy spots, and their importance goes past their tasteful allure.

They are viewed as wellsprings of life, immaculateness, and profound association. The tropical charm of fog in Tahiti, as it touches the cascades, turns into a festival of the harmonious connection among nature and culture, where fog turns into a medium through which the sacrosanct is uncovered.

Reef Puzzler: Hazy Enchantment in Fiji's Coral Nurseries

Wandering further into the Pacific, we show up in Fiji, a tropical heaven eminent for its coral nurseries and completely clear waters. Here, the tropical charm of fog takes on an oceanic structure, as fog transcends the coral reefs like a mystical cloak. The stories of foggy wizardry in Fiji's coral nurseries uncover a captivating exchange between the warm tropical air and the energetic submerged biological systems.

The fog over Fiji's coral reefs is certainly not a simple meteorological event; it is a demonstration of the complicated connections among land and ocean. The fog conveys with it minuscule particles that act as supplements for the coral, adding to the wellbeing and dynamic quality of the submerged biological systems. The tropical charm of fog in Fiji turns into a biological dance, where the fog turns into a fundamental player in the fragile equilibrium of life underneath the waves.

Mysterious Rainforests: Vanua Levu's Cryptic Shelter

In the Fijian archipelago, the fog stretches out its tropical appeal to the rainforests of Vanua Levu, making a confounding shade that cover the verdant scenes. Vanua Levu, the second-biggest island in Fiji, is home to lavish rainforests where fog floats through the thick foliage, uncovering stories of biodiversity and environmental wealth. The enchanted rainforests, covered in fog, harbor endemic species and make an environment where life flourishes in an orchestra of tropical rhythms.

The fog in Vanua Levu's rainforests isn't only climatic; it is a help for the different vegetation that call these tropical shelters home. The dampness conveyed by the fog feeds the vegetation and supports a mind boggling snare of life, from dynamic orchids to slippery birds. The stories of magical rainforests in Vanua Levu divulge the interconnectedness of fog, rainforest biological systems, and the fragile equilibrium that characterizes the tropical charm of this Pacific island objective.

Social Dream: Fog in the Legends of Samoa

In Samoa, fog takes on social dream, meshing itself into the legends and customs of the islands. The tropical charm of fog in Samoa is profoundly implanted in the social texture, where fog isn't simply a climate peculiarity yet a divine element with stories to tell. The stories of fog in

Samoa unfurl as social accounts that associate individuals to the land, ocean, and sky.

In Samoan folklore, fog is frequently connected with profound creatures, including the goddess of the mist, Nafanua. Fog turns into a scaffold between the natural and the heavenly, with social services and customs respecting the presence of this divine substance. The tropical charm of fog in Samoa is consequently in excess of an air event; it is a social respect for the mysterious characteristics of fog, where the shroud between the seen and the concealed turns out to be slender, welcoming the occupants to embrace the ethereal excellence inside their social legacy.

Island Murmurs: Fog in the Marquesas Archipelago

As we excursion to the Marquesas Archipelago, a confined heaven in French Polynesia, the tropical charm of fog takes on a wonderful pith. The Marquesas, described by sensational scenes and taking off volcanic pinnacles, frequently ends up hidden in fog that adds a fleeting quality to its charm. The stories of fog in the Marquesas unfurl as island murmurs, where fog turns into a narrator, covering and uncovering the forms of these far off islands.

In the Marquesan culture, fog is praised as an idyllic power that improves the excellence of the scenes. The cloudy cover become a similitude for the transient idea of life, where the ethereal nature of fog reflects the transitory minutes that characterize presence. The tropical charm of fog in the Marquesas turns into an encouragement to mull over the interconnectedness of nature, culture, and the immortal magnificence that covers these disconnected islands in a cloak of fog.

Protection Congruity: Shielding the Tropical Appeal

In the midst of the stories of fog in Pacific island objections, a pivotal story arises — the congruity between tropical charm and preservation endeavors. The delicacy of these hidden heavens requests a guarantee to reasonable practices, natural stewardship, and a significant regard for the sensitive biological systems that characterize the tropical charm of the Pacific.

Preservation drives, whether zeroed in on safeguarding fog loaded rainforests, protecting coral reefs, or advancing eco-accommodating the travel industry, are urgent parts of uncovering the drawn out supportability of these tropical objections. As fog assumes a crucial part in the environmental equilibrium, defending the tropical charm requires an all encompassing methodology that thinks about both the seen and concealed parts of these island biological systems.

Revealing the Hidden Marvels of the Pacific

In the tropical appeal of fog, Pacific island locations unfurl as hidden delights with stories to tell. From fog enveloped mountains by Hawaii to flowing cloak in Tahiti, from cloudy sorcery in Fiji's coral nurseries to mysterious rainforests in Vanua Levu, every objective uncovers an exceptional exchange among nature and culture. Fog becomes a climatic event as well as a social, biological, and tasteful power that characterizes the charm of these paradisiacal domains.

As we finish up our investigation of fog in Pacific island locations, the greeting is clear — to embrace the hidden wonders, to pay attention to the narratives conveyed by the fog, and to become stewards of the sensitive biological systems that add to the tropical appeal. The Pacific, with its fog loaded scenes, allures explorers and progressives the same to divulge the secrets inside the shroud, guaranteeing that these heavens persevere for a long time into the future. The tropical charm of fog in the Pacific is a consistently developing orchestra, where the hidden excellence keeps on moving wonderment, respect, and a guarantee to safeguarding the charm inside the cloudy hug of these perfect islands.

6.2 Exploring misty jungles, volcanic landscapes, and hidden waterfalls.

Investigating Foggy Wildernesses, Volcanic Scenes, and Secret Cascades: An Excursion into Nature's Privileged insights

Leaving on an excursion into the core of dim wildernesses, volcanic scenes, and secret cascades is to step into a domain where nature uncovers its most complex privileged insights. This investigation takes us across assorted biological systems, from rich wildernesses hidden in fog to the crude magnificence of volcanic territories, disclosing the secret ponders that characterize these scenes. As we adventure further, the stories of fog, volcanic magnificence, and flowing cascades unfurl, each portraying an account of regular wonders ready to be found.

Hazy Wildernesses: The Cryptic Cover of Borneo

Borneo, a verdant island shared by Malaysia, Indonesia, and Brunei, coaxes with fog covered wildernesses that harbor a cryptic marvel. As we dive into the core of these hazy wildernesses, a rich embroidery of biodiversity unfurls. The stories of fog in Borneo uncover the air appeal as well as the environmental meaning of the hidden scenes.

The fog that wraps the wildernesses of Borneo is a critical component supporting the lavish vegetation and different untamed life. It goes about as a characteristic hydrator, wrapping the thick foliage with dampness that upholds a heap of plant and creature species. Fog turns into the imperceptible string associating the various layers of the biological system, from transcending trees to subtle animals that flourish in the damp hug of the wilderness. The investigation of foggy wildernesses in Borneo is a submersion into the many-sided dance of life, where each bead of fog adds to the dynamic quality of this enrapturing biological system.

Volcanic Magnificence: Iceland's Extraordinary Landscape

Iceland, a land etched by the basic powers of fire and ice, reveals an alternate feature of nature's privileged insights — volcanic magnificence. The Icelandic scene, described by volcanic cavities, fountains, and magma fields, is a demonstration of the land ponders that lie underneath the World's surface. As we cross the supernatural territory molded by volcanic movement, stories of base powers and dynamic scenes arise.

The volcanic scenes of Iceland, frequently hung in fog and encompassed by an enchanted feel, convey accounts of Earth's essential power. The stories of volcanic greatness uncover the geographical cycles that have formed the island over centuries. Fog, ascending from geothermal vents and underground aquifers, adds an ethereal quality to the volcanic territory. It turns into a visual orchestra, where the juxtaposition of fog and distinct volcanic highlights makes a stunning scene that addresses the crude excellence and geographical show of Iceland's consistently evolving scenes.

Flowing Murmurs: Cascade Mysteries in the Amazon Rainforest

The Amazon Rainforest, a rambling wild that envelops various nations in South America, disguises quite possibly of nature's generally captivating mystery — secret cascades. As we explore through the thick foliage of the rainforest, the flowing murmurs of cascades call, uncovering stories of detached excellence and biological importance. These secret cascades, frequently covered in fog, become asylums where the rainforest divulges its mysteries.

The stories of cascades in the Amazon Rainforest are stories of nurturing waters and environmental availability. These flowing miracles add to the mind boggling hydrological pattern of the rainforest, supporting the rich biodiversity that calls this biological system home. The fog that encompasses the cascades adds a dash of secret, veiling the fountains in an ethereal sparkle. Investigating these secret cascades is a submersion into the biological concordance of the Amazon, where the murmurs of falling water become a tune in the ensemble of the rainforest.

Supernatural Coverings: Costa Rica's Cloud Timberlands

Costa Rica, a Focal American pearl, is prestigious for cloud timberlands — supernatural shades transcend the tropical scenes. As we climb into these high-height domains, stories of dim charm and biodiversity unfurl. The cloud woodlands of Costa Rica are hidden in never-ending fog, making an environmental milieu that sustains an extraordinary collection of verdure.

The fog that covers Costa Rica's cloud woodlands is a characterizing highlight, impacting the environments in significant ways. It gives a nonstop inventory of dampness to the vegetation, supporting an overflow of orchids, greeneries, and epiphytes that stick to the branches. The stories of magical overhangs uncover the fragile harmony among fog and biodiversity, where the ethereal cover become a life saver for endless species adjusted to the high-height conditions. Investigating Costa Rica's cloud woodlands is an excursion into the core of dim biological systems, where each step disentangles the privileged insights concealed inside the whirling fogs.

Volcanic Cover: Hawaii's Mauna Kea and Mauna Loa

Hawaii, a tropical heaven in the Pacific, flaunts foggy wildernesses as well as volcanic shroud that shape its famous scenes. Mauna Kea and Mauna Loa, two transcending volcanoes on the Enormous Island, uncover stories of volcanic grandness hidden in fog.

These giant pinnacles, frequently covered with snow, are topographical marvels as well as social and profound milestones.

The fog that covers Mauna Kea and Mauna Loa adds a layer of persona to these volcanic goliaths. In Hawaiian folklore, these pinnacles are viewed as sacrosanct, and fog is frequently connected with the presence of otherworldly substances. The volcanic cloak become a material where social stories and normal magnificence combine. Investigating the fog loaded slants of these volcanoes is a drenching into the crossing point of topography and otherworldliness, where the inconspicuous powers shape both the physical and supernatural parts of Hawaii's volcanic scenes.

Secret Fountains: New Zealand's Fiordland

New Zealand's Fiordland, a district of sensational fjords and rough scenes, covers stowed away fountains that add to its charm. As we explore the coves, stories of fog loaded cascades uncover themselves, making a climate of eminent excellence. Fiordland's secret fountains, frequently took care of by precipitation and fog, overflow down steep bluffs, making an orchestra of water and fog that reverberations through the fjords.

The stories of stowed away fountains in New Zealand's Fiordland address the unique transaction between weather conditions and the normal geography. Fog, conveyed by winds that scope across the Tasman Ocean, turns into a groundbreaking power, making transient cover that wrap the cascades. Investigating these secret fountains is an excursion into the core of Fiordland's topographical show, where fog becomes both the craftsman and the narrator in the consistently developing story of water and rock.

Hidden Charm: Indonesia's Bromo Tengger Semeru Public Park

Indonesia, a rambling archipelago, is home to Bromo Tengger Semeru Public Park — a domain of hidden charm where fog, volcanic scenes, and secret cascades meet. Mount Bromo, a functioning well of lava, ascends from an ocean of fog, making a supernatural display that enthralls the faculties. The stories of hidden charm in this public park unfurl as a visual orchestra, where fog turns into the ethereal cloak that changes the volcanic scenes into a domain of strange magnificence.

The fog that covers Bromo Tengger Semeru Public Park isn't simply a climate peculiarity; an extraordinary component adds a layer of charm to the volcanic landscape. As the fog whirls around the holes and magma fields, it turns into a quiet dance accomplice to the unique powers that have molded this scene over ages. Investigating this hidden charm is an encouragement to observe the agreeable exchange among fog and volcanic greatness, where nature's mysteries are divulged in each wisp of haze.

Nature's Embroidered artwork Revealed

Our investigation of hazy wildernesses, volcanic scenes, and secret cascades, it becomes obvious that nature's embroidered artwork is woven with strings of secret and miracle. Every location, from Borneo's dim wildernesses to Iceland's volcanic magnificence, from the Amazon Rainforest's secret cascades to New Zealand's Fiordland, adds to a story where the concealed cloak become basic to the excellence and biological concordance of the scenes.

The investigation of fog, volcanic scenes, and cascades isn't simply an actual excursion; it is an excursion into the embodiment of nature's privileged insights. It is an affirmation that, past the noticeable magnificence, there are stories scratched in the fog, geographical wonders etched by volcanic powers, and flowing cascades that murmur stories of environmental interconnectedness. As we dig into these scenes, we become observers to the unfurling story of our planet, where each foggy shroud, volcanic pinnacle, and secret fountain adds to the stupendous orchestra of nature's embroidery — a consistently developing magnum opus ready to be investigated and treasured.

6.3 Cultural stories of mist as a bridge between nature and spirituality.

Social Accounts of Fog: A Scaffold Among Nature and Otherworldliness

In different corners of the world, social stories have woven stories of fog into the actual texture of customs, making a scaffold between the substantial excellence of nature and the elusive domain of otherworldliness. These accounts, went down through ages, lift fog from a meteorological peculiarity to a holy substance, interfacing networks to the scenes they occupy and the otherworldly aspects they venerate. As we dig into these social stories, we leave on an excursion where fog turns out to be something other than an environmental event; it turns into a channel for the greatness of the human soul into the persona of the regular world.

Covered Tranquility: Japanese Feel and the Mysterious Kiri

In the Place that is known for the Rising Sun, Japan, fog isn't just a weather pattern; it is a fundamental piece of the country's tasteful way of thinking. The Japanese expression for fog, "kiri," holds social importance that goes past its visual appeal. Kiri is frequently connected with tranquility, secret, and the transient idea of presence. The social accounts of fog in Japan unfurl as stories of covered quietness, where kiri turns into an illustration for the fleetingness of life and the magnificence tracked down in brevity.

In customary Japanese craftsmanship and writing, fog is habitually portrayed as a groundbreaking power that obscures the limits between the material and profound domains. Fog covered scenes, like those around Mount Fuji, are commended for their ethereal excellence, welcoming thought and reflection. The social hug of fog in Japan is a demonstration of the significant association among nature and otherworldliness, where the hidden scenes become a material for the lovely articulation of the human spirit.

Divine Fumes: Antiquated Greek Folklore and the Emanation of Nyx

In the old woven artwork of Greek folklore, fog takes on divine importance through the figure of Nyx, the goddess of the evening. Nyx, whose very substance is wrapped in the hazy fumes of night, turns into an extension between the human world and the heavenly domains. The social accounts of fog in old Greece weave a story of extraordinary magnificence and the groundbreaking force of the evening.

Nyx, frequently depicted as a hidden figure rising up out of the fog, typifies the persona and profundity of the nighttime hours. The fog turns into her emanation, a divine shroud that shrouds the earth in murkiness and clues at the mysteries of the universe. In the social accounts of old Greece, fog rises above the commonplace to turn into an image of the heavenly, where the ethereal idea of Nyx's presence in the night sky brings out a feeling of miracle and respect for the secrets outside human ability to comprehend.

Hallowed Fogs: Native Viewpoints in North America

Across the huge scenes of North America, native societies have developed a profound relationship with the land, and fog is many times seen as a consecrated indication of the World's breath. The social accounts of fog among native networks address a significant comprehension of nature's interconnectedness with otherworldliness. Fog isn't just a climate peculiarity however a living presence, an otherworldly power that wraps the earth in its hug.

In Local American customs, fog is viewed as an edge between the physical and otherworldly domains. It is during the foggy minutes, as first light breaks or night plunges, that the cloak between universes is accepted to be slim. The narratives of sacrosanct fogs portray the presence of familial spirits, creature guides, and heavenly energies that manifest in the ethereal magnificence of the fog. In this social setting, fog turns into a medium through which correspondence with the otherworldly aspects is worked with, manufacturing a profound and sacrosanct connection between native networks and the normal world.

Hidden Sanctuaries: Hinduism's Profound Association with Vaporous Components

In the rich embroidery of Hinduism, fog tracks down its place in the regular scene as well as inside the sacrosanct engineering of sanctuaries. The social accounts of fog in Hindu practices investigate the otherworldly meaning of vaporous components, especially during customs and functions. Fog turns into an image of virtue and heavenly presence, connecting the earthly with the divine in an agreeable dance.

In Hindu sanctuaries, where customs are performed to interface with the heavenly, fog is frequently connected with the contribution of incense and the consuming of sacrosanct spices. The rising fumes are viewed as a course for supplications, conveying the goals of admirers to the sky. The social association among fog and otherworldliness is complicatedly woven into the texture of Hindu customs, where the ethereal magnificence of fog turns into a substantial articulation of dedication and the hallowed idea of the environmental elements.

Mysterious Hazes: Celtic Practices and the Extraordinary Domain

In the fog loaded scenes of Celtic customs, fog isn't simply a meteorological event; a shroud isolates the human domain from the powerful. The social accounts of fog in Celtic legends are packed with stories of enchanted mists that act as passages to domains past human discernment. Fog turns into an edge, a liminal space where the unremarkable and the mysterious join.

Celtic folklore frequently depicts fog as an extraordinary component, disguising stowed away ways and charmed lands. In accounts of faeries, spirits, and old divinities, fog turns into the supernatural shroud that permits these mysterious creatures to cross between universes concealed. The social hug of fog in Celtic customs mirrors a profound regard for the secrets of nature and the conviction that, inside the hidden scenes, one can get looks at the remarkable.

Divine Murmurs: Buddhism's Insightful Association with Air Cover

In the pensive customs of Buddhism, fog turns into an illustration for the temporariness of presence and the transient idea, everything being equal. The social accounts of fog in Buddhist way of thinking are permeated with a feeling of thoughtful reflection, welcoming specialists to consider the fleeting magnificence of the climatic cover. Fog, in this specific circumstance, turns into an educator, murmuring significant bits of insight about the idea of the real world.

Buddhist craftsmanship frequently portrays fog as an ethereal component that encompasses edified creatures, representing their amazing quality past the material world. The narratives of heavenly murmurs in Buddhist customs investigate the pensive association with fog as a vehicle for profound knowledge. Fog, with its momentary nature, turns into a visual indication of the fleetingness that underlies all parts of presence, empowering specialists to develop care and separation.

Otherworldly Fumes: African Animism and the Presence of Hereditary Spirits

In the animistic customs of different African societies, fog is viewed as a sign of profound powers, especially the presence of tribal spirits. The social accounts of fog in African animism mirror a significant association between the regular components and the profound aspects that shape the perspective of these networks. Fog, or otherworldly fumes, is viewed as an unmistakable articulation of the concealed powers that impact the natural domain.

In customs and services, fog is much of the time deciphered as an indication of the presence of genealogical spirits or gods. The tales of profound fumes describe minutes when fog slips upon sacrosanct locales, representing a fellowship between the living and the spirits of the withdrew. Fog turns into a course for profound energies, a peculiarity that spans the unmistakable and elusive, producing a profound feeling of solidarity between the actual world and the otherworldly aspects.

Of fog as a scaffold among nature and otherworldliness, a consistent idea arises — the acknowledgment of fog as a bringing together substance that rises above social and geological limits. These different accounts highlight the widespread human propensity to look for associations with the normal world and to track down profound importance in the components that encompass us.

Interconnected Insight: A Worldwide Embroidery of Fog

As we cross the globe from the perspective of social stories, it becomes clear that fog isn't bound to a particular locale or conviction framework. All things considered, a worldwide peculiarity gets a scope of reactions from various societies, each adding to a rich embroidery of interconnected shrewdness. Whether it's the otherworldly kiri in Japan, the heavenly fumes of Nyx in old Greece, or the profound fumes in African animism, fog turns into an image of the transaction between the natural and the heavenly.

The worldwide embroidery of fog uncovers a common human encounter — a natural longing to grasp the secrets of presence and to produce associations with the concealed. In societies all over the planet, fog fills in as a representation for the shroud that isolates the known from the obscure, welcoming examination and respect for the unutterable parts of life.

Otherworldly Imagery: Fog as an Illustration for Life's Excursions

Social accounts of fog frequently use it as an illustration for life's excursions — both physical and profound. The fleeting idea of fog, its inclination to show up and disperse, mirrors the transient nature of human life. In Japanese feel, fog addresses the excellence found in temporariness, provoking a more profound appreciation for the brief minutes that characterize our lives.

Essentially, in Celtic customs, fog fills in as an image of change and change. It turns into the barometrical medium through which one can navigate from the ordinary to the otherworldly, epitomizing the possibility that life is an excursion loaded up with secrets and disclosures. The representative reverberation of fog in social accounts mirrors the general human mission for importance and grasping despite life's inborn temporariness.

Sacrosanct Biology: Fog as a Gatekeeper of Nature's Holiness

Numerous social stories view fog as a gatekeeper of nature's holiness, stressing the hallowed environment that exists between the regular world and otherworldly domains. Native points of view in North America perceive fog as an edge where the profound and actual aspects entwine. Fog turns into a sacrosanct presence, working with a fellowship with hereditary spirits and typifying the interconnectedness of every living being.

In Hindu customs, fog in sanctuaries isn't simply an environmental peculiarity yet a sacrosanct sign. The rising fumes are viewed as a sacrosanct contribution, conveying the requests and goals of admirers to the heavenly domains.

Fog turns into a medium through which the holiness of the sanctuary is raised, associating the earthbound with the divine in an agreeable connection between the sacrosanct and the normal.

Shrewdness in Brevity: Fog as an Educator in Buddhist Way of thinking

Buddhist way of thinking sees fog as an instructor, offering significant illustrations about the idea of presence. Fog's transient and fleeting nature turns into a similitude for the temporariness, everything being equal. In the scrutinizing customs of Buddhism, fog murmurs experiences about the passing excellence of life and the significance of developing care in each second.

The narratives of fog in Buddhist societies urge experts to embrace the insight tracked down in brevity. Fog turns into a delicate suggestion to relinquish connections, to live completely in the present, and to perceive the temporariness that underlies the texture of presence. Along these lines, fog turns into a profound aide, encouraging people to set out on an excursion of self-disclosure and illumination.

Harmonious Congruity: Fog as a Connector of Nature and Otherworldliness

Across different societies, fog fills in as a connector, manufacturing harmonious concordance between the domains of nature and otherworldliness. In Japan, fog represents the association between the substantial and elusive, featuring the excellence that arises when these domains converge. Fog turns into a scaffold, welcoming people to consider the fragile dance between the seen and the inconspicuous.

In the Amazon Rainforest, fog associates the earthbound with the profound in native points of view. Dim minutes are viewed as holy, making a space where the cloak between universes become flimsy. Fog turns into a channel for correspondence with genealogical spirits, epitomizing an amicable connection between the regular world and the profound aspects.

Social Strength: Fog as a Wellspring of Motivation and Veneration

Social accounts of fog likewise uncover its job as a wellspring of motivation and versatility. In Samoa, fog is respected as a heavenly element, meshing itself into the texture of social stories. Fog turns into a wellspring of motivation for services and customs, representing the persevering through flexibility of the Samoan nation notwithstanding life's difficulties.

Essentially, fog in Celtic practices turns into an image of flexibility and versatility. Hazy scenes are not deterrents but rather pathways to charmed domains, showing the social strength implanted in stories that track down excellence and enchantment even amidst vulnerability.

Fog, A General Cover of Association

In the heap social accounts of fog, a well known fact arises — fog is in excess of a meteorological peculiarity; a cloak associates humankind to the consecrated, the supernatural, and the regular.

Whether covered in the stylish way of thinking of Japan, hidden in the fantasies of old Greece, or entwined with the otherworldly acts of native societies, fog turns into a widespread image that rises above topographical and social limits.

Social stories of fog, with their different viewpoints and translations, welcome people to participate in a common exchange with the normal world. Fog turns into a general cloak that joins networks in respect for the concealed, the otherworldly, and the transient idea of life. In the narratives of fog, mankind tracks down a typical language — a language that addresses the significant interconnectedness of all things and the sacrosanct magnificence that lies past the noticeable shroud of the normal world.

Chapter 7

Ancient Mysteries of Asian Temples

Old Secrets of Asian Sanctuaries: Revealing Otherworldly Quality

In the core of Asia, where revered customs meet with significant otherworldly convictions, antiquated sanctuaries stand as persevering through landmarks to the secrets that have dazzled ages. These asylums, frequently shrouded in the fogs of time, demonstrate the veracity of the rich embroidery of Asian societies, lodging inside their hallowed walls the perplexing stories and otherworldly wonder that have molded the locale's set of experiences. As we leave on an excursion to disclose the old secrets of Asian sanctuaries, we dive into the domains where engineering, workmanship, and otherworldliness merge, uncovering stories that rise above the restrictions of time.

India's Sanctuaries: Reverberations of Godliness in Stone

In the huge field of India, a land saturated with otherworldliness and different conviction frameworks, sanctuaries are more than simple structural wonders — they are living declarations to the country's profound association with the heavenly.

From the many-sided carvings of Khajuraho to the transcending towers of Varanasi, every sanctuary portrays a remarkable story, an impression of the diverse strict texture woven across the subcontinent.

The old secrets of Indian sanctuaries lie in their capacity to epitomize the embodiment of astronomical request and heavenly agreement. In Khajuraho, the unpredictably cut figures portray scenes of regular daily existence, entwined with heavenly creatures took part in divine demonstrations. The sanctuaries become consecrated fenced in areas where the limits between the natural and the heavenly break down, welcoming admirers and guests the same to think about the everlasting dance of creation and obliteration.

Varanasi, on the banks of the hallowed Ganges Stream, is home to sanctuaries that reverberation with the serenades of explorers and the reverberation of old ceremonies. The secret lies in the coherence of love, a solid chain that stretches across hundreds of years. The Ghats of Varanasi, embellished with sanctuaries committed to different divinities, become stages where life, demise, and otherworldliness meet in a scene that rises above the material domain.

Angkor Wat: Cambodia's Engineering Ensemble

In the thick wildernesses of Cambodia, the titanic sanctuaries of Angkor Wat stand as a demonstration of the magnificence of the Khmer Domain. The old secrets installed inside the unpredictably cut stone walls and transcending towers of Angkor Wat unfurl as an ensemble of design, otherworldliness, and cosmology.

Underlying the twelfth 100 years, Angkor Wat was devoted to the Hindu god Vishnu before later changing into a Buddhist sanctuary. Its plan reflects the vast request, with the focal pinnacle representing Mount Meru, the grandiose hub. The bas-reliefs describe sagas and legends, welcoming the individuals who cross its corridors to set out on a visual and profound excursion through time.

Angkor Wat's puzzling arrangement with divine peculiarities during huge cosmic occasions adds one more layer to its mystery. The sanctuary's direction towards the west, frequently connected with death in Hindu cosmology, alludes to the mind boggling associations between life, passing, and the grandiose cycles implanted in the actual texture of this structural wonder.

Borobudur: Indonesia's Astronomical Mandala in Stone

Indonesia's Borobudur, settled in the lavish scenes of Java, is a titanic Buddhist stupa that unwinds the secrets of vast request and edification. Built in the ninth 100 years, Borobudur is a demonstration of the building ability of the Sailendra tradition and the profound vision that motivated its creation.

The construction of Borobudur mirrors an inestimable mandala, a many-sided mathematical plan addressing the universe. As pioneers climb its numerous porches, they leave on a representative excursion towards Nirvana, directed by complicated help boards portraying the life and lessons of Buddha. The culmination, delegated with stupas, represents the fulfillment of edification.

The antiquated secrets of Borobudur lie in its compositional plan as well as in its otherworldly imagery. The reconciliation of Buddhist cosmology, ceremonial practices, and imaginative articulation makes a consecrated space that rises above the limits of time. Borobudur remains as a landmark to the quest for higher information and the timeless mission for profound arousing.

Shwedagon Pagoda: Myanmar's Overlaid Reference point of Otherworldliness

In the core of Yangon, Myanmar's Shwedagon Pagoda rises wonderfully, its brilliant tower gleaming in the daylight. As quite possibly of the holiest Buddhist site in the country, the old secrets of Shwedagon Pagoda are saturated with legend, otherworldliness, and the getting through commitment of the Myanmar public.

Rumors from far and wide suggest that Shwedagon Pagoda cherishes relics of four Buddhas, making it a worshipped journey site. Its overlaid surface, decorated with jewels and other valuable stones, mirrors the dedication of ages who have added to its adornment. The focal stupa, coming to towards the sky, represents the pivot of the universe in Buddhist cosmology.

The secrets of Shwedagon Pagoda stretch out past its actual structure. The customs, celebrations, and the ardent explorers who circle base add to a quality of otherworldliness pervades the air. As the daylight washes the pagoda in a brilliant shine during dusk, it turns into a reference point that rises above the material world, welcoming examination and veneration.

Taktsang Palphug: Bhutan's Tiger's Home Religious community

Roosted on the edge of a precipice in the Paro Valley of Bhutan, Taktsang Palphug, or Tiger's Home Cloister, typifies the otherworldly levels to which commitment can rise. The antiquated secrets of this cloister lie in its problematic area as well as in the legends that encompass its starting point.

Rumors have spread far and wide suggesting that Master Rinpoche, a worshipped figure in Bhutanese Buddhism, traveled to this area on the rear of a tigress, reflecting in a cavern that would later become Taktsang Palphug. The religious community, developed around this hallowed site, is a demonstration of the harmonious connection between the otherworldly and normal universes.

The climb to Tiger's Home includes a trip across flawless timberlands and steep paths, adding a layer of actual test to the profound excursion. Travelers and guests the same participate in the old secrets of Taktsang Palphug, seeing a combination of building magnificence and the profound energies that have pervaded the site for quite a long time.

Horyu-ji: Japan's Living Tradition of Buddhism

In the tranquil scenes of Nara, Japan, Horyu-ji remains as a living demonstration of the acquaintance of Buddhism with the island country. Laid out in the mid seventh 100 years, Horyu-ji is perhaps of the most established wooden design on the planet and houses a variety of curios that mirror the development of Buddhist workmanship and culture in Japan.

The antiquated secrets of Horyu-ji unfurl through its engineering format and the fortunes inside its regions. The five-story pagoda, an image of enormous solidarity, remains close by the primary corridor, lodging sculptures and relics that follow the improvement of Buddhist iconography in Japan. The pagoda's focal support point is said to contain remains of Buddha, adding a layer of holiness to its construction.

Horyu-ji's importance lies in its verifiable significance as well as in its job as a storehouse of Buddhist lessons and relics. The antiquated secrets implanted inside its wooden walls welcome thought on the getting through tradition of Buddhism in Japan and the profound reverberation that keeps on reverberating as the centuries progressed.

7.1 Concluding the journey with the mystical mists surrounding Asian temples.

The supernatural fogs encompassing Asian sanctuaries, similar to a delicate shroud, add an ethereal aspect to the otherworldly embroidery woven by these old designs. As we finish up our excursion through the consecrated grounds of India's sanctuaries, Cambodia's Angkor Wat, Indonesia's Borobudur, Myanmar's Shwedagon Pagoda, Bhutan's Tiger's Home Cloister, Japan's Horyu-ji, and other hallowed locales, the exchange between magic, engineering, and otherworldliness turns out to be perpetually evident.

In the Baffling Hug of Fog:

Fog, with its tricky nature, rises above the unmistakable and blends consistently with the otherworldly vibe of Asian sanctuaries. In the fog covered scenes of India, where antiquated structures reverberation the serenades of enthusiasts, and the etched divinities appear to rise out of the mist, the heavenly and the barometrical merge. The strange fog encompassing Cambodia's Angkor Wat adds a powerful quality to the generally remarkable sanctuary complex, changing it into a domain where the past and the current dance together in the hidden hug of history.

The antiquated secrets of Asian sanctuaries, elevated by the cover of fog, stretch out to Indonesia's Borobudur, where the stone stupas appear to rise out of the ethereal domain. The transaction of light and fog at the crack of dawn reveals a visual ensemble, doing magic that rises above the transient. In Myanmar, the brilliant tower of Shwedagon Pagoda penetrates through the fog, making a divine exhibition that reverberates with the otherworldly dedication of the people who journey to its consecrated grounds.

Fog as an Otherworldly Impetus:

Bhutan's Tiger's Home Cloister, roosted problematically on the edge of a bluff, turns into a guide rising up out of the spiritualist mists, coaxing travelers on an excursion that rises above actual difficulties. The whirling fog turns into a profound impetus, wrapping the cloister in a quality of greatness. In the tranquil scenes of Japan's Horyu-ji, fog loans a demeanor of immortality to the old wooden designs. The pagoda, the primary lobby, and the encompassing nurseries become baffling domains where the limit between the holy and the normal breaks up.

Imagery in the Whirling Shroud:

Past the visual display, fog in Asian sanctuaries conveys significant imagery. It turns into a similitude for the transient idea of presence, repeating the Buddhist standards of temporariness. The fog that shrouds the old designs is an update that, similar to the haze disseminating with the morning sun, life is fleeting, and everything is dependent on future developments. The fog turns into a representative cover, hiding and uncovering, welcoming consideration on the secrets that lie past the material world.

The Consecrated and the Magnificent:

The holiness of Asian sanctuaries is raised to the wonderful when embraced by fog. The hidden climates bring out a feeling of secret, as though the godliness inside the sanctuary edifices conveys through the whirling mists. In Bhutan, as pioneers rise towards the Tiger's Home, the fog turns into a quiet buddy, murmuring the insight of the mountains and the mysteries of the profound excursion.

In Japan, the fog wreathed halls of Horyu-ji radiate a quietness that rises above time. The wooden designs, lodging old ancient rarities and sacrosanct relics, become vessels of otherworldly reverberation, resounding with the embodiment of Japanese Buddhism. The glorious excellence of Asian sanctuaries, increased by fog, turns into a channel for a more profound association with the heavenly and a thoughtful fellowship with the secrets of presence.

A General Shroud:

The persona of fog encompassing Asian sanctuaries is a general peculiarity. It rises above social and geological limits, winding around a repeating theme that interfaces these sacrosanct destinations. Whether it is the murky mornings in Kyoto, where the fog cover the torii entryways of Fushimi Inari Place of worship, or the unpretentious cover that folds over the old stupas of Bagan in Myanmar, fog turns into a general shroud that joins different profound practices.

The antiquated secrets implanted in the engineering, figures, and ceremonies of these sanctuaries find reverberation in the barometrical cover that encompass them. Fog turns into a quiet narrator, describing stories of commitment, design virtuoso, and the persevering through journey for the hallowed. It is a general language spoken in the murmurs of the breeze through sanctuary patios, in the delicate footfalls of explorers rising sacrosanct advances, and in the ethereal dance of haze around old towers.

The Agelessness of Custom:

As we finish up our excursion through the magical fogs encompassing Asian sanctuaries, the immortality of custom arises as a focal subject. The antiquated secrets are not relics of the past but rather living stories, went down through ages. The fog, with its capacity to change the everyday into the mysterious, turns into a similitude for the persevering through nature of these practices.

In India, where the fog embraces the sanctuaries of Khajuraho, the old secrets persevere in the customs performed by ministers and the veneration of fans. The compositional wonders of Angkor Wat in Cambodia, when hidden in fog, transport guests to when Khmer lords looked for divine blessing through stupendous developments. The fog turns into an extension across hundreds of years, interfacing the contemporary with the old, welcoming consideration on the recurrent idea of custom.

A Continuum of Otherworldliness:

The supernatural fogs encompassing Asian sanctuaries are not stale substances but rather part of a continuum of otherworldliness. They wrap these consecrated spaces in a steadily evolving dance, representing the ease of the otherworldly excursion. In Borobudur, where fog entwines with the stone reliefs, the ageless lessons of Buddha track down articulation in the transient magnificence of the climate.

The fog turns into a representation for the consistently present otherworldly quintessence that rises above fleeting imperatives. In Bhutan, as the fog grips to the precipices around Tiger's Home Cloister, the continuum of commitment is tangible. Explorers, continuing in the strides of their precursors, add to the continuous story of otherworldliness, each step reverberating with the antiquated secrets cherished in the cloister's establishments.

Embracing the Mysterious Shroud

The mysterious fogs encompassing Asian sanctuaries act as shroud that both hide and uncover the antiquated secrets inside. They intensify the holiness of these spaces, lifting them to domains where the profound and the normal unite. Whether it's the twirling hazes in the sanctuaries of Kyoto, the foggy day breaks in Varanasi, or the ethereal climates of Borobudur, the fog turns into a graceful articulation of the significant association among humankind and the heavenly.

As we navigate the scenes of custom, otherworldliness, and structural wonders, the fog arises as a bringing together component — a quiet observer to the getting through journey for the consecrated. It welcomes us to mull over the immortal stories carved in stone, the customs performed through hundreds of years, and the secrets that continue through the ages. Embracing the enchanted cover of fog, we find ourselves within the sight of old sanctuaries as well as within the sight of something otherworldly — a profound quintessence that rises above both time and fog, interfacing us to the everlasting.

7.2 Examining the symbolic and spiritual significance of mist in Asian cultures.

Investigating the Ethereal: The Emblematic and Otherworldly Meaning of Fog in Asian Societies

In the complicated dance between the earthly and the supernatural, fog arises as a quiet hero, projecting an ethereal spell across the scenes of Asian societies. Past its meteorological job, fog expects significant emblematic and otherworldly importance, winding around an embroidery that joins the domains of nature, folklore, and human otherworldliness. As we leave on a scrutinizing venture, we dig into the fog loaded stories of Asia, where the inconspicuous transaction of mist turns into an emblematic language, resounding with the shared mindset of different social orders.

Fog as the Cover of Secret:

In the social dictionary of Asia, fog frequently expects the job of a spiritualist cover, covering scenes in a cryptic emanation that welcomes examination. This imagery is well established in the possibility of disguise and disclosure, where fog turns into the ethereal drapery between the known and the unexplored world. Whether encompassing the old sanctuaries of Angkor Wat or wandering through the bamboo woodlands of Kyoto, fog projects a groundbreaking cover, hoisting the normal to the exceptional.

This imagery reverberations in the dim scenes of Indian otherworldliness, where the Ganges Stream wanders through the blessed city of Varanasi. As the fog ascends from the consecrated waters, it turns into a representation for the hidden edges among life and demise, the seen and the concealed. The ghats of Varanasi, enhanced with fog, encapsulate a liminal space where the commonplace and the profound meet, offering looks into the secrets that rise above the material domain.

Fog and Brevity:

Integral to the otherworldly methods of reasoning of Asia is the idea of temporariness, and fog fills in as a strong visual illustration for the transient idea of presence. In Japan, fog is embraced in the social stylish of "Mono no Mindful," the consciousness of temporariness and the excellence of short lived minutes. Here, fog loaded scenes, similar to those encompassing Mount Fuji, become living articulations of the temporariness that underlies all parts of life.

The imagery of fleetingness is especially piercing in Bhutan, where the Tiger's Home Cloister roosts on a precipice, frequently darkened by fog. The temporary perceivability of the religious community in the midst of the twirling mists reflects the temporariness of the actual world, welcoming reflection on the vaporous idea of life and the profound excursion towards edification.

Profound Immaculateness and Purging:

Fog, with its relationship with water drops and the purifying properties of dampness, turns into an image of profound virtue and cleansing across Asian societies. This imagery is profoundly imbued in customs and customs where water, as fog, is utilized as a refining specialist. In Hinduism, the fog kissed streams and lakes are not just water bodies but rather consecrated domains where sanitization ceremonies unfurl.

In Myanmar, the brilliant tower of Shwedagon Pagoda, hidden in morning fog, turns into a sacrosanct seal of immaculateness. The fog, in this specific situation, is certainly not a simple climate peculiarity however a profound specialist that sanctifies the environmental factors, making an air where lovers participate in refining customs, both physical and otherworldly.

The Edge to the Heavenly:

Asian societies frequently see fog as an edge to the heavenly, a medium through which the natural and the divine domains meet. This representative understanding is profoundly implanted in the legends and otherworldly stories that paint fog as a course for divine energies. In Hinduism, fog is related with the heavenly breath, an ethereal appearance that associates the human with the godlike.

The fog covered scenes of Bali, Indonesia, where old sanctuaries rise up out of the haze, support this thought of fog as a limit. The hidden sanctuaries become asylums where the heavenly and the natural combine, and fog turns into the representative cover that isolates the standard from the holy. This liminal space welcomes admirers to rise above the material world and draw in with the numinous aspects past.

The Ethereal Dance of Yin and Yang:

In Chinese way of thinking, fog encapsulates the unique transaction of Yin and Yang, the restricting yet correlative powers that shape the universe. The foggy scenes of conventional Chinese ink artworks, where mountains rise up out of twirling mists, encapsulate this amicable dance of contrary energies. Fog turns into the visual portrayal of the repeating idea of presence, where light and shadow, lucidity and lack of definition, entwine in a vast artful dance.

This representative duality is apparent in the fog covered terraced fields of Guilin, where the scene changes into a supernatural domain. The fog, in this unique situation, isn't just climatic dampness yet a sign of the fragile harmony between contradicting powers.

It turns into a visual sonnet that addresses the everlasting dance of congruity and differentiation, repeating the significant philosophical underpinnings of Chinese culture.

Watchmen of Nature's Holiness:

In native societies across Asia, fog is much of the time apparent as a gatekeeper of nature's sacredness, a living presence that typifies the interconnectedness of the normal and the profound. This imagery is profoundly implanted in animistic convictions, where fog isn't simply a climate peculiarity however an otherworldly power that wraps the earth in its hug. In the cloudy scenes of the Amazon rainforest, where old trees are hidden in haze, native networks see the fog as a sacrosanct element.

Fog turns into a middle person between the human and soul universes, a peculiarity that works with fellowship with hereditary spirits and heavenly energies. This social point of view considers fog to be an exemplification of the holiness intrinsic in the biodiversity and biological systems of the area. In this specific situation, fog turns into a substantial articulation of the concealed powers that shape the normal world, producing a profound feeling of solidarity between the physical and the otherworldly aspects.

An Impetus for Consideration:

Fog, with its fleeting and tricky nature, fills in as an impetus for thought in the otherworldly acts of Asia. The dim scenes become scrutinizing spaces where people take part in contemplation and look for a more profound association with the heavenly. In the fog loaded woodlands of Japan, where Shugendo specialists leave on austere excursions, fog becomes both the physical and allegorical cover that prompts profound experiences.

Likewise, in the dim domains of the Himalayas, where yogis and searchers take part in reflective practices, fog turns into a medium that uplifts the thoughtful experience. The whirling mists that encompass mountain tops make a climate helpful for consideration, welcoming people to dig into the profundities of their cognizance and associate with the extraordinary parts of presence.

Past the Cover of Imagery:

The emblematic and profound meaning of fog in Asian societies rises above its job as a meteorological peculiarity. Fog turns into a language, an image, and a conductor for the significant profound stories that unfurl across different scenes. From the hazy sanctuaries of Kyoto to the ethereal domains of the Himalayas, the hidden scenes become consecrated materials whereupon social, fanciful, and profound stories are painted.

Fog, in its complex imagery, welcomes people to peer past the shroud of the material world and draw in with the unspeakable elements of presence. It turns into an indication of temporariness, an image of virtue, a limit to the heavenly, and an impetus for consideration.

The fog loaded stories of Asia coax us to not simply notice however to take part in the ageless dance between the seen and the concealed, where the cloak of fog become scaffolds to the profound domains that rise above both time and culture.

7.3 Reflecting on the echoes of mist across diverse continents.

Reverberations of Fog Across Different Landmasses: An Intelligent Excursion

In the peaceful murmurs of the normal world, fog arises as a widespread peculiarity that rises above geological limits, encompassing different landmasses in its ethereal hug. From the fog covered scenes of the Scottish Good countries to the cryptic shroud of the Himalayas, every mainland tells its special story of fog, winding around a story that reverberations through reality. As we set out on an intelligent excursion, we investigate the common and particular characteristics of fog across mainlands, revealing the strings that interface humankind to the persona of the inconspicuous.

The Magical Cover of Scottish Fogs:

In the old scenes of Scotland, fog turns into a magical cover that covers the moving slopes, old palaces, and quiet lochs. The reverberations of fog in Scotland are profoundly woven into the social texture, making a barometrical scene that resounds with legends and fables. As fog twists around the tough pinnacles of the High countries and floats over the peaceful waters of Loch Ness, it turns into a living substance, encapsulating the actual pith of Scottish magic.

The fog in Scotland is in excess of a weather condition; it is a narrator, projecting a shroud over verifiable stories and legends. In the remnants of middle age palaces, fog turns into the ethereal friend of old spirits, waiting in the air like murmurs from a past period. The reverberations of fog in Scotland, with its combination of normal excellence and social legacy, summon a feeling of immortality, welcoming reflection on the interconnectedness of history and nature.

Himalayan Levels: Covers of Otherworldly Nepal:

As we climb to the great levels of the Himalayas, fog assumes an alternate personality, turning into a heavenly cover that wraps the transcending pinnacles of Nepal. The reverberations of fog in Nepal resound with otherworldliness and wonderment, winding around a story of worship for the holy levels. The cloudy mornings in the Himalayas become a ceremonial divulging, where each layer of haze uncovers the old mysteries concealed in the folds of the mountains.

In the profound embroidery of Nepal, fog isn't simply a meteorological event; it is a heavenly peculiarity. The rising fumes become a contribution, climbing from the earthbound domain to the heavenly home. Fog in the Himalayas epitomizes the exchange between the natural and the otherworldly, making a climate where petitioning heaven banners shudder in the concealed flows and where religious communities roost on bluffs like ethereal asylums. The reverberations of fog in Nepal resound with the journey for otherworldly levels, coaxing travelers and searchers to navigate the hazy paths in quest for illumination.

Stories of the Amazon: Perplexing Rainforests of Brazil:

Wandering into the core of the Amazon rainforest, fog takes on an alternate pretense — a lavish and puzzling cloak that covers the biodiversity-rich scenes of Brazil. The reverberations of fog in the Amazon confess to stories of stowed away mysteries, of a flourishing environment disguised inside the ringlets of haze. As fog winds through the transcending trees and moves over the crooked streams, it turns into a quiet narrator of the harmonious connection among nature and the native networks that call the rainforest home.

In the Amazonian stories, fog isn't simply an environmental peculiarity; a living element shapes the actual quintessence of the rainforest. It turns into a fundamental power in the pattern of life, supporting the verdure that rely upon its feeding contact. The reverberations of fog in the Amazon resonate with the interconnectedness of every single living being, advising us that inside the whirling mist lies the unpredictable snare of life that supports the planet.

Sahara's Quiet Sands: Unwinding the Confounding Fogs:

In the tremendous spread of the Sahara Desert, fog unfurls as an uncommon and mysterious guest, changing the quiet sands into a vaporous exhibition. The reverberations of fog in the Sahara recount accounts of inconsistency — an apparently fruitless scene showing some signs of life with the dash of haze. As fog floats over the rises and shroud the old scenes, it turns into an update that even in the most bone-dry conditions, nature winds around its own stories of flexibility and transformation.

The fog in the Sahara is a demonstration of the desert's capacity to disguise and uncover. It turns into a painter, embellishing the rises with transient strokes of dampness, abandoning hints of life in the apparently forlorn scopes. The reverberations of fog in the Sahara resound with the calm murmurs of endurance, where vegetation adjust to the steadily changing elements of a scene that changes from dried to fruitful with the appearance of haze.

Icy Murmurs: Frozen Secrets of Scandinavia:

In the furthest reaches of Scandinavia, fog takes on a frigid structure, enclosing the Icy scenes by a frozen hug. The reverberations of fog in the Cold recount accounts of chilling magnificence, where chilly shroud cloak fjords and icy masses in a dance of ethereal polish. Fog, in the Cold stories, turns into a quiet ally toward Aurora Borealis, a tricky accomplice in the hypnotizing divine artful dance that graces the polar skies.

In the Icy's frozen murmurs, fog turns into a middle person between the unmistakable scenes and the supernatural lights that enlighten the polar evenings. It changes frosty territories into domains of charm, where fog and snow team up to make a tranquil dreamscape. The reverberations of fog in Scandinavia resound with the sensitive harmony between brutal real factors and the delicate excellence that arises when the Cold scenes are kissed by the breath of mist.

Pacific Islands: Hidden Heavens Disclosed:

As we cross the Pacific Islands, fog appears as a hidden heaven, a wonderful presence that improves the charm of tropical scenes. The reverberations of fog in the Pacific Islands tell stories of stowed away cascades, fog kissed wildernesses, and volcanic territories where haze winds through the rich overhangs. In these paradisiacal domains, fog turns into a creative associate, improving the visual verse of palm-bordered sea shores and emerald-green scenes.

In the stories of the Pacific Islands, fog is an unpretentious craftsman, making a material where the shades of nature are mellowed and mixed into an amicable range. It turns into the buddy of morning dews and delicate downpours, sustaining the dynamic environments that flourish in the hug of Pacific fogs. The reverberations of fog in these heavens murmur of the fragile biological systems that depend on the transient dash of haze, cultivating a significant association between the islands and the normal powers that shape them.

Social Stories Across Landmasses:

As we ponder the reverberations of fog across different mainlands, it becomes obvious that fog isn't simply a meteorological event yet a social peculiarity. It is a quiet storyteller, winding around stories of folklore, otherworldliness, and the multifaceted connections among people and the normal world. Whether it is the fog covered palaces of Scotland, the otherworldly levels of the Himalayas, the energetic biological systems of the Amazon, the immense deserts of the Sahara, the frozen secrets of Scandinavia, or the paradisiacal scenes of the Pacific Islands, fog is a basic piece of the social woven artwork.

Fog, in its different structures, welcomes thought on the widespread topics that associate humankind across landmasses. It turns into an update that, underneath the variety of scenes and societies, there exists a common appreciation for the mysterious, the inconspicuous, and the transient magnificence that arises when haze entwines with the shapes of the Earth. The reverberations of fog rise above topographical limits, turning into a widespread language that resounds with the shared mindset of mankind.

The Baffling Dance of Fog: A Continuum of Nature's Stories

As we dig further into the confounding dance of fog, our process keeps on unfurling, uncovering the complexities and subtleties that characterize the connection among humankind and the vaporous cover that shroud our reality. Past the topographical scenes, fog turns into an immortal go between, directing us through a continuum of nature's stories that rise above mainlands and ages. Each murmur of haze conveys with it the reverberations of old stories, social engravings, and the significant interconnectedness that ties us to the inconspicuous.

In the Strides of Old Palaces: A Scottish Dream:

Scotland, with its fog covered fields and old palaces, remains as a demonstration of the persevering through charm of the baffling. The reverberations of fog in the Scottish High countries resound with the strides of history, where legends are woven into the actual texture of the scene.

In the shadow of middle age strongholds, fog turns into the ethereal ally to stories of knights and apparitions, each twirl of haze covering and uncovering the secrets that wait in the air.

As we cross the environmental scenes of Scotland, fog turns into a narrator, painting the heather-shrouded slopes with a range of secret. The social reverberation of fog in Scotland reaches out past the visual scene; it is imbued in the Good country customs, where the ethereal nature of haze turns into an image of flexibility, reflecting the getting through soul of a land molded by fantasy and history.

Himalayan Levels: Pinnacles Penetrating the Shroud:

Climbing to the magnificent levels of the Himalayas, the dance of fog takes on a profound importance, turning into a scaffold between the natural and the heavenly. The reverberations of fog in Nepal resound with the serenades of priests and the strides of travelers rising holy pinnacles. Fog turns into an illustration for the greatness of the material world, a peculiarity that mellow the rough edges of hilly scenes, making a climate where the unremarkable converges with the mysterious.

In the Himalayan accounts, fog turns into the quiet observer to the otherworldly excursions of the people who look for illumination. The twirling mists that hide old cloisters and petitioning God banners become a visual song, reverberating through the valleys and gulches. Fog, in the Himalayas, turns into an educator, welcoming reflection on the fleeting ness of life and the timeless journey for higher conditions of cognizance.

Amazonian Insider facts: Foggy Rainforests of Brazil:

Wandering into the core of the Amazon rainforest, fog uncovers its mysteries in the rich hug of biodiversity. The reverberations of fog in the Amazon resonate with the energetic life that flourishes underneath its hidden shade. As haze winds through the thick foliage, it turns into a custodian of the insider facts concealed inside the green embroidery — a keeper that welcomes us to investigate the secrets of one of the most biodiverse biological systems on The planet.

Fog, in the Amazonian stories, isn't simply a climatic peculiarity; it is a gatekeeper of old insight. Native viewpoints divulge fog as an other-worldly power, a living element that interfaces humankind with the throbbing heartbeat of the rainforest. It turns into an image of the sensitive harmony between human life and the many-sided snare of life, an equilibrium that is unendingly kept up with inside the twirling fogs of the Amazon.

Saharan Murmurs: Secrets in the Sands:

As we cross the limitlessness of the Sahara Desert, the perplexing dance of fog becomes the dominant focal point in a scene apparently lifeless. The reverberations of fog in the Sahara tell stories of versatility and variation, where haze turns into a groundbreaking power in a climate described by limits. Fog, in the Sahara, challenges predispositions, uncovering that even in the cruelest of conditions, life figures out how to thrive when moved by the breath of haze.

The Sahara turns into a material where fog paints transient strokes of life on the sandy region. In this bone-dry wild, fog turns into a stone carver, forming the rises and uncovering the perplexing impressions of animals that explore the quiet sands. The Sahara's murmurs in the fog entice us to reexamine our view of devastation and embrace the strength implanted in the core of one of the world's most famous deserts.

Cold Murmurs: Frozen Secrets of Scandinavia:

In the Cold span of Scandinavia, fog unfurls as a quiet observer to the frozen secrets that beauty polar scenes. The reverberations of fog in the Cold tell stories of distinct magnificence, where chilly cover dance over fjords and icy masses, making a climate of peaceful charm. Fog, in Scandinavia, turns into an associate toward Aurora Borealis, a heavenly exhibition that enlightens the polar evenings in a stunning presentation.

As we explore the chilling excellence of fog in Scandinavia, it turns into an illustration for the sensitive harmony between unforgiving real factors and the delicate charm of the Icy. Fog turns into the creative brushstroke that mellow the forms of frigid scenes, transforming frozen landscapes into ethereal domains. In the Cold murmurs of fog, we find a nuanced story that challenges our impression of destruction and divulges the peaceful strength of life in outrageous environments.

Pacific Islands: Hidden Heavens Uncovered:

Venturing to the Pacific Islands, fog arises as a hidden heaven, an inconspicuous power that improves the charm of tropical scenes. The reverberations of fog in the Pacific Islands weave stories of stowed away cascades, fog kissed wildernesses, and volcanic territories where haze entwines with rich overhangs. Fog turns into a creative partner, molding the visual verse of palm-bordered sea shores and emerald-green scenes.

In the Pacific Islands' stories, fog turns into the delicate touch that supports energetic environments, encouraging a sensitive harmony among widely varied vegetation. The reverberations of fog in these paradisiacal domains resound with the social stories that praise the personal association between the islands and the normal powers that shape them. Fog, in the Pacific, is a demonstration of the agreeable concurrence of mankind and the rich conditions that characterize these tropical Edens.

Social Stories Across Mainlands:

As we consider the reverberations of fog across different landmasses, a typical topic arises — the crossing point of nature and culture. Fog, in its different structures and signs, turns into a general image that rises above topographical limits, welcoming consideration on our common human experience. Whether it is the fog covered palaces of Scotland, the otherworldly levels of the Himalayas, the dynamic biological systems of the Amazon, the Sahara's quiet sands, the frozen scenes of Scandinavia, or the paradisiacal domains of the Pacific Islands, fog turns into a similitude for the inconspicuous powers that shape our reality.

Social stories entwine with the reverberations of fog, making a rich embroidery where human stories and regular peculiarities meet. Fog turns into the quiet storyteller of history, fantasy, and otherworldliness — a vessel through which social engravings are conveyed across ages. Every mainland, with its novel scenes and social subtleties, adds to the always advancing discourse among mankind and the secrets hid inside the folds of haze.

The Inconspicuous Continuum:

The puzzling dance of fog unfurls as a continuum of nature's stories, interfacing landmasses and societies in a consistent embroidery. Fog, in its ethereal excellence, turns into a widespread language that resounds with the human spirit. Whether it is the old reverberations in the Scottish fields, the otherworldly murmurs of the Himalayan levels, the biodiversity-rich privileged insights of the Amazon rainforest, the secrets hid in Sahara's sands, the frozen marvels of Scandinavia, or the paradisiacal charm of the Pacific Islands, fog fills in as a quiet scaffold between the seen and the concealed.

As we explore the reverberations of fog across different landmasses, we find that inside the whirling shroud lies a common appreciation for the otherworldly, the transient, and the significant. Fog turns into an illustration for the elusive powers that shape our reality, an update that past the noticeable scenes, there exists a continuum of stories that rise above existence. In the dance of fog, we track down the magnificence of the concealed as well as the implicit discourse among humankind and the regular world — an exchange that rises above landmasses, reverberating through the shared perspective of our planet.